Assisted Reproduction in Israel

Family Law in a Global Society

Editor-in-Chief

Sanford N. Katz (*Boston College*)

Associate Editors

Masha Antokolskaia (*VU University Amsterdam*)
Bill Atkin (*Victoria University of Wellington*)
Ursula C. Basset (*Pontificia Universidad Católica Argentina*)
Linda Elrod (*Washburn University School of Law*)
Ann Laquer Estin (*The University of Iowa College of Law*)
Jonathan Herring (*Exeter College, University of Oxford*)
Robin Fretwell Wilson (*University of Illinois College of Law*)
Jinsu Yune (*Seoul National University School of Law*)

Volumes published in this Brill Research Perspectives title are listed at *brill.com/rpfl*

Assisted Reproduction in Israel

Law, Religion and Culture

By

Avishalom Westreich

BRILL

LEIDEN | BOSTON

This paperback book edition is simultaneously published as issue 1 (2) 2016, in *Family Law in a Global Society*, DOI 10.1163/24058386-12340002.

Library of Congress Control Number: 2018932215

Typeface for the Latin, Greek, and Cyrillic scripts: "Brill". See and download: brill.com/brill-typeface.

ISBN 978-90-04-34606-2 (paperback)
ISBN 978-90-04-34607-9 (e-book)

This book is printed on acid-free paper and produced in a sustainable manner.

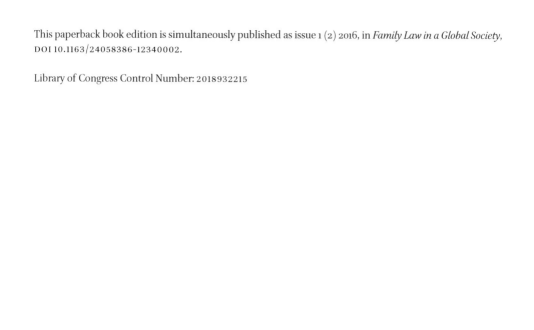

Contents

Assisted Reproduction in Israel: Law, Religion and Culture

Avishalom Westreich
Associate Professor of Law, College of Law and Business, Ramat Gan;
Research Fellow, Shalom Hartman Institute, Jerusalem, Israel
avishalomw@clb.ac.il

Abstract

The theme of this composition is the right to procreate in the Israeli context. Our discussion of this right includes the implementation of the right to procreate, restrictions on the right (due to societal, legal, or religious concerns), and the effect of the changing conception of the right to procreate (both substantively and in practice) on core family concepts.

In the current Israeli legal and cultural sphere, two issues are at the forefront of the discussion over the right to procreate: first, the regulations governing and conflicts surrounding surrogacy and egg donation, and second, the debate over posthumous fertilization. The first, surrogacy and egg donation, is the typological modern expansion

* Ph.D., M.A. (Hermeneutic Studies); B.A. (History; Talmud); L.L.B. (Law). Associate Professor, College of Law and Business, Ramat Gan, Israel; Research Fellow, Kogod Research Center for Contemporary Jewish Thought, Shalom Hartman Institute, Jerusalem; Helen Gartner Hammer Scholar-in-Residence, Hadassah-Brandeis Institute, Brandeis University (Fall 2016); Visiting Scholar, Petrie-Flom Center for Health Law Policy, Biotechnology, and Bioethics, Harvard Law School (Fall 2017).

I am grateful to these institutions for providing me with the opportunity to conduct the research upon which this work is based. Special thanks to my colleagues and friends at the Jewish Law Research Group at Hartman Institute for the opportunity to discuss and share ideas, to I. Glenn Cohen and the participants of the Petrie-Flom Center's Scholars and Students Fellows Workshop for their excellent comments on Part 2, and to Sanford Katz for initiating and encouraging this project. I also wish to thank Tzivya Beck and Kalila Courban for their research assistance and Edward Levin for his thoughtful linguistic editing.

 | DOI 10.1163/9789004346079_002

of, or alternative to, traditional procreation. It opens the gates of procreation to individuals and couples for whom natural procreation was not possible in the past (due to medical reasons, sexual orientation, etc.), while, at the same time, it challenges the very understanding of fundamental family practices and concepts, especially as regards parenthood, motherhood, and fatherhood. *Part 1* of this composition accordingly discusses the right to procreate, focusing on the regulation and practice of surrogacy and egg donation in Israel.

The second issue, posthumous procreation, is an excellent illustration of the expansion of the right to procreate, and a typological example of how this expansion moderates, or even blurs, existential dichotomies, such as life and death. *Part 2* therefore discusses posthumous fertilization, with a focus on the debate over posthumous sperm retrieval of fallen soldiers. This debate clarifies the conceptual distinction between an individual right to procreate and a communal, or familial, right to continuation, along with the fascinating tension between the legal system and the social and political atmospheres.

On the basis of the first two parts, *Part 3* focuses on the dramatic conceptual changes of parenthood definitions resulting from the evolution of assisted reproductive technologies (ART) and from the broadening of the right to procreate (both are, of course, related, and influence each other). This part deals with the move from formal to functional parenthood, both in Israeli civil law and in Jewish law. The perspective of Jewish law is a significant player at this field, and it is discussed in various occasion throughout this composition. *Part 4* accordingly completes the discussion by providing some description and analysis of the basic Jewish law approaches to ART.

To sum up, the main argument in this composition is that assisted reproduction in Israel gives expression to and develops the right to procreate. It is a complex right, and therefore at times no consensus has been reached on the form of its actual application (as in the case of surrogacy and egg donation, and, from a different direction, in that of posthumous sperm retrieval). This right, however, despite the debates on its boundaries, is widely accepted, practiced, and even encouraged in the Israeli context, with a constructive collaboration of three main elements: the Israeli civil legal system, religious law (which in the context of the Israeli majority is Jewish law), and Israeli society and culture.

Keywords

egg donation – surrogacy – artificial insemination – posthumous fertilization – postmortem sperm retrieval – Jewish law – Israeli law – parenthood – fatherhood – motherhood – family law – bioethics – law and religion

Introduction

Discussing assisted reproduction in general, and in Israel in particular, is quite challenging. This broad topic includes multiple issues, diverse methods, and a broad spectrum of viewpoints. Moreover, the legal field, to which this work belongs, is in dynamic and intensive interaction with other fields, such as the scientific or social fields, which affect its potential content as well. The structure of such a composition, its course, and its objectives should take into account the multiple parameters of the subject, and difficult choices of what to include and what to omit must be made.

What issues should be part of such a discussion? We could focus on a systematic discussion of various assisted reproductive technologies (ART): classic in vitro fertilization (IVF) which uses the intended parents' gametes, or the more complex IVF procedures, such as surrogacy and egg donation; technologies related to reproduction, such as preimplantation genetic diagnosis procedure (PGD) and mitochondrial replacement; posthumous sperm retrieval; and others. In this context, an issue-oriented discussion could deal with legal restrictions on these technologies, the implications of these technologies for individuals, families, and society, their development, and the challenges they pose.

Alternatively, we could examine comprehensive social, cultural, normative, bioethical, or religious aspects that emerge from the discussion of assisted reproduction, rather than a systematic technology-oriented perspective. This might include the very right to procreate and its application, for example: the right of same-sex couples for procreation, and the need of same-sex male couples (in the Israeli context) to use international surrogacy (and the problematic outcomes of this option, such as the commercialization of women's bodies in developing countries). No less an important, challenging, and fascinating issue is posthumous fertilization, which includes both considerations of the social and personal consequences of this technology, and normative and bioethical questions of the right of others to initiate and perform posthumous procreation.

There is, therefore, a wide range of possible issues within the broad topic of ART in Israel, one quite different from the other. Discussing assisted reproduction, however, is not merely a matter of the issues themselves. One great challenge of any author in general, and regarding this topic in particular, is the method used for his or her writing. Should we choose a descriptive discussion of assisted reproduction in Israel? The great advantage of this kind of discussion is that it provides the reader with a sweeping and accurate picture of the topic. But it is not always possible to maintain one's detachment from such a highly sensitive issue. Therefore, the author might choose a normative approach, in which her or his main object is to indicate, on the basis of an analysis of various aspects of the current situation, the main weaknesses or defects of the current arrangements, and to propose structural and contentual alternatives. A normative method could contribute greatly to the topic (and to society and its legal system), although it might be unavoidably biased. A third possible method for this kind of study is historical. Assisted reproduction is a dramatically developing topic. Scientific revolutions influence society and its norms. They change society's perceptions of some of its central components, such as family, parenthood, and even life and death. Needless to say, this directly affects its legal system, and—perhaps surprisingly—it might also influence one of the central and sacred elements of a society—its religion. A researcher with a historical perspective on this matter might seek to reveal developmental processes, analyze cultural and conceptual changes, and discuss the multiple interactions within society and their influence on society's concepts over the course of time.

Thus, we have various possible issues to discuss and methods by which these issues might be examined, and of course—almost any combination of these options might be used. The dilemmas, however, do not end here. Any author has his or her own viewpoint. Should this affect the content of the research, its course, or its conclusions? Is it possible at all to avoid this influence, and compose an agendaless work? Let us examine this dilemma as regards ART. A functionalist approach might emphasize the social structures that encourage ART, or the degree to which ART is incorporated in existing social (cultural, religious, etc.) circumstances. A critical approach could seek to reveal the social inequality that ART promotes, or the suppressive elements that are hidden in current ART policy (against women, homosexuals, those living in developing countries, etc.). A feminist viewpoint (either classic or radical) would focus on ART's effect on women, a religious viewpoint would carefully analyze the results of ART from the point of view of a religious legal system, and so on.

Actually, legal writing, especially of the kind in which I engage, is interpretative. The last dilemma is therefore the classic issue of the influence of an individual's point of view (or prejudice, or bias) on his or her interpretation. This is a classic hermeneutical question, which goes far beyond the topic under discussion here, and even far beyond the legal discipline as a whole. Obviously, we cannot resolve this in the current work (if it can be resolved at all). In a somewhat paradoxical way, this weighty question assists me, as a writer, to make choices regarding the three elements that were mentioned in the beginning of this introduction: the issues discussed, the methodology, and the possible influence of the author's viewpoint.

My hermeneutical starting point is a moderate one, that strives for the greatest possible objectivity in the interpretative process, on the one hand, while nevertheless acknowledging that any interpretation is colored, in some degree, by the interpreter's world. The interpretative process, however, is not all that is liable to be influenced: the choice of the issues to be examined and the methods employed in these discussions, too, are not immune to such factors. Thus, for example, my interpretation of the legal reality in Israel as regards ART includes more references to the Jewish law aspects of this topic (as compared to other scholars), which I have extensively explored, and might even give expression in a greater degree to religious law concepts (some critics might argue that my writing, is influenced by my own point of view too, which I try to avoid). The balance and decisions regarding the three: issues, method, and viewpoint, are, in fact, the classic fusion of horizons of the text and the interpreter (using Hans-Georg Gadamer's terminology). This fusion influences the writing in various degrees, as mentioned, and the fashioning of the composition.

What, then is the rationale behind the topics and methods I have chosen? The theme of this book is the right to procreate in the Israeli context. Our discussion of this right includes the implementation of the right to procreate, restrictions on the right (due to societal, legal, or religious concerns), and the effect of the changing conception of the right to procreate (both substantively and in practice) on core family concepts, such as parents, father, and mother.

Defining the theme of this book as the right to procreate still leaves some decisions to be taken. Boundaries must be delineated for this extremely broad topic. In my opinion, in the current Israeli legal and cultural sphere, two issues are at the forefront of the discussion over the right to procreate: first, the regulations governing and conflicts surrounding surrogacy and egg donation, and second, the debate over posthumous fertilization.

The first, surrogacy and egg donation, is the typological modern expansion of, or alternative to, traditional procreation. It opens the gates of procreation to individuals and couples for whom natural procreation was not possible in the past (due to medical reasons, sexual orientation, etc.), while, at the same time, it challenges the very understanding of fundamental family practices and concepts, especially as regards parenthood, motherhood, and fatherhood. Sperm donation (and artificial insemination by donor) does the same, in some respect, but is closer to traditional, biological, procreation, and thus the conflicts and challenges that it raises are not as pronounced as those relating to surrogacy and egg donation.

Part 1 of this book will accordingly discuss the right to procreate, focusing on the regulation and practice of surrogacy and egg donation in Israel. It will discuss the current legal arrangements, and analyze the recent debates in these matters, mainly, the right of same-sex couples to use surrogacy and egg donation, and the justification for the demand for genetic connection between the intended parents and the child, in order to legally approve these technologies. Conflicts and questions concerning artificial insemination by donor, or matters related to surrogacy and egg donation which are not at the heart of the right to procreate, will not be discussed independently, but rather as part of our central focus: the Israeli legal arrangement of surrogacy and egg donation, with its difficulties and challenges.

The second issue which stands at the forefront of the right to procreate discussion is posthumous procreation. This, in my opinion, is an excellent illustration of the expansion of the right to procreate, and a typological example of how this expansion moderates, or even blurs, existential dichotomies, such as life and death. By postmortem sperm retrieval a dead man can become a parent when his sperm is used to impregnate a living woman, creating a post-life continuation for himself. No doubt, this penetration of living elements to death—"life after death"—is a significant change in our notion of the absoluteness of life and death. It raises social, bioethical, and religious concerns, alongside a dramatic conceptual change.

Part 2 will therefore discuss posthumous fertilization, with a focus on the debate over posthumous sperm retrieval of fallen soldiers. This debate clarifies the conceptual distinction between an individual right to procreate and a communal, or familial, right to continuation, along with the fascinating tension between the legal system and the social and political atmospheres.

Part 3 will focus on the dramatic conceptual changes of parenthood definitions resulting from the evolution of assisted reproductive technologies and from the broadening of the right to procreate (both are, of course, related, and influence each other). This part deals with the move from formal to functional parenthood, which characterizes the common family law discourse today, in Israel and abroad. On this basis, the part discusses the relationship between civil law and Jewish law and the mutual effect of this relationship on parenthood definitions. It shows how civil law's functional approach carefully considers the view of religious law ("considerate functionalism"), and reveals a fascinating four-stage move of Jewish law from substantive to functional parenthood.

Part 4 will complete the discussion by providing some description and analysis of the basic Jewish law approaches to ART. The subject of this work is ART in Israel, rather than Jewish law, but since the perspective of Jewish law is a significant player at this field, and since it is discussed in various occasion throughout this composition, I have chosen to conclude this composition with the necessary background, that would supplement some possible gaps, which could not be expanded in other parts.

The latter leads me to clarify a significant point as regards to ART in Israel. The subtitle of this monograph is: "Law, Religion, and Culture." These three elements represent in my view the dominant factors that shape ART in Israel. Indeed, as discussed in the beginning of this introduction, the weight of each one of the three, and even the very choice of these three elements as the central elements of ART, is a hermeneutical choice resulting from various factors, including the author's background. I am aware that this kind of a discussion could have been conducted elsewise, with a different weight given to each element. For example, even by accepting these three as the main elements in ART in Israel, the discussion could focus on the patriarchal views that are reflected in them, on the social structures that shape them, and the like. I, however, will focus on the functional contribution of the three, separately and jointly. I view the three as highly influential as regards the right to procreate, and as elements which are themselves shaped in the mutual interaction between them. That is, civil law influences and is influenced by religious law, religious law influences and is influenced by civil law, and both are a reflection of the culture of the given society in which they exist.

To sum up, my main argument in this book is that assisted reproduction in Israel gives expression to and develops the right to procreate. It is a complex right, and therefore at times no consensus has been reached on the form of its actual application (as in the case of surrogacy and egg donation, and, from a different direction, in that of posthumous sperm retrieval). No less importantly, this is an essential right within Israel's dynamic society. It has a dramatic effect on the central family concepts of parenthood and parent-child relations, and in general, it impacts on social, legal, and religious perceptions of the family itself.

Part 1 The Right to Procreate in Surrogacy and Egg Donation: Legal Arrangements, Difficulties, and Challenges

I *Background*

What makes Israel a superpower of assisted reproduction? Procreation has a central place in Israeli society and culture, and that leads to the intensive use of assisted procreation. A few factors influence this phenomenon, starting with religious and cultural ties to the Biblical commandment to "be fruitful and multiply" (Genesis 1:28) which might be seen as pronatalist positions, and ending with a deep consciousness among the Jewish part of Israeli society of the need for the rehabilitation of the Jewish people after the Holocaust.[1] This goes together with a highly modernized medical system, which provides a growing number of couples and singles with the option to use assisted reproductive technologies.

Opposite factors, however, that restrain the use of ART are also present. The traditionality of large parts of Israeli society (Jewish and non-Jewish alike), together with the significant power of the religious establishment in both the political and legal spheres, limit the use of ART, especially when these technologies are required for non-traditional families, such as homosexual couples and singles.

This tension is highly important in framing the nature of ART in Israel. Let us explore it a little bit further. On the one hand, Israel is quite open in permitting a wide range of reproductive technologies and procedures, including some which are prohibited in many other Western countries. For example, the law permits paid surrogacy;[2] the law permits egg donation, including the combination of egg donation and surrogacy;[3] postmortem sperm retrieval was approved by the Supreme Court when the process is initiated by the deceased's spouse.[4] Some of these procedures are limited, or completely restricted, in other Western countries.[5] It seems, when focusing on the permitting aspects, that there are very powerful forces that encourage the Israeli legal and health system to widen the use of assisted reproduction. This is especially so as regards more traditional assisted reproduction procedures. The fact that the

1 *See* references *infra*, note 7. As an introductory anecdotal remark, I would like to add the following observation. In a private talk with Prof. Ami Amit (the head and founder of the central IVF clinic in Ichilov Medical Center, Tel Aviv, and the founder of a few IVF centers in Israel and all over the world), Amit explained his motivation to promote IVF as a direct result of the devastation caused by the Holocaust ("we are lacking 6,000,000 people," in his words; although, of course, his contribution to human procreation crosses nations and faiths). Amit defined himself as an "absolutely secular" Jew, thus distinguishing between the Holocaust motivation and other traditional pronatalist factors (a private talk with Prof. Amit, Harvard Law School, November 3, 2017; I thank Rabbi Hirschy Zarchi of Chabad at Harvard for making this conversation possible).

2 *See* Embryo Carrying Agreements Law (Approval of the Agreement and the Status of the Child), 5756–1996 (*henceforth*: Embryo Carrying Agreements Law), Section 6.

3 Egg Donation Law, 5770–2010 (*henceforth*: Egg Donation Law), section 6(b).

4 *See* Family Appeal Request 7141/15 Plonit v. Plonit et al. (December 22, 2016) (Heb.) (Isr.); and *see infra*, Part 2.

5 *See*, e.g., *infra*, Part 2, note 2.

Israeli national health insurance funds in vitro fertilization procedures for women under 45 is a result of those forces, and a catalyst for widening the use of ART. To demonstrate this: the Israeli media reported that the number of IVF procedures in Israel increased in 2016 by 11% compared to 2015, and by more than 40% compared to 2014.[6] Not surprisingly, the use of IVF in Israel is among the highest in the world.[7]

On the other hand, there are legal restrictions on nontraditional families and general restrictions due to religious considerations. For example, surrogacy is permitted in Israel only for heterosexual couples, while same-sex couples who wish to procreate need to use international surrogacy.[8] The law also limits procreation with the assistance of a third party (egg donation or surrogacy) to a third party who belongs to the same religion as that of the intended parents (although in exceptional cases it is possible to bypass this requirement).[9] Matters of personal status are adjudicated in Israel according to the religion of the parties, and religion and religious status in Israel are culturally meaningful and legally important. Although this legal situation is the subject of debate in Israel, and there are voices that call for change,[10] the legislator did not intend to harm this structure when dealing with ART. Therefore, the legislator retains religious sectarianism. In addition, the legislator emphasizes that the laws that deal with ART would not influence the decisions of marriage and divorce

6 *See* Ido Efrati, "Israel Remains an IVF Paradise as Number of Treatments Rises 11% in 2016," HAARETZ, May 11, 2017 (http://www.haaretz.com/israel-news/.premium-1.788244; accessed July 4, 2017).

7 *See* Carmel Shalev and Sigal Gooldin, *The Uses and Misuses of In Vitro Fertilization in Israel: Some Sociological and Ethical Considerations*, 12 NASHIM: A JOURNAL OF JEWISH WOMEN'S STUDIES AND GENDER ISSUES 151 (2006). On the problematic aspects of this situation, *see* Yehezkel Margalit, *Scarce Medical Resources—Parenthood at Every Age, In Every Case and Subsidized By the State?*, 9 NETANYA ACAD. L. REV. 191 (2014) (Heb.). For a shorter English version, *see* Yehezkel Margalit, *Scarce Medical Resources? Procreation Rights in a Jewish and Democratic State* (2011), http://ssrn.com/abstract=1807908 (unpublished manuscript); For a forceful normative argument against the (international) rise of the use of assisted reproduction instead of the adoption of already-born children (both national and international adoption) *see* Elizabeth Bartholet, *Intergenerational Justice for Children: Restructuring Adoption, Reproduction and Child Welfare Policy*, 8 LAW & ETHICS HUM. RIGHT 103 (2014), and the literature cited *id.*

8 *See* the definition of "intended parents" in the Embryo Carrying Agreements Law, Section 1: "a man and a woman who are a couple."

9 *See* Embryo Carrying Agreements Law, Section 2(5); Egg Donation Law, Section 13(c)(e)(3)–(4).

10 *See* AVISHALOM WESTREICH & PINHAS SHIFMAN, A CIVIL LEGAL FRAMEWORK FOR MARRIAGE & DIVORCE IN ISRAEL (Ruth Gavison, ed., Kfir Levy, trans., 2013).

matters, which are made according to religious law, and thereby prevents any apparent conflict.

What, then, is the character of the right to procreate in the Israeli legal system? The complicated, somewhat challenging, situation described above leads to a complex right to procreate. As will be explored in this part, the right exists, with restrictions, and is subject to a continuing process of expansion. We will discuss this argument through an analysis of two paradigmatic assisted reproductive technologies: surrogacy and egg donation.

II *Surrogacy and Egg Donation: Restricted Openness*

The Israeli legal system was one of the first to regulate egg donation and surrogacy. Progress is made from time to time in modifying those regulations, along with continuing legal and public struggles for their expansion.[11] As mentioned, the current legal arrangements are both open and restricted regarding the use of surrogacy and egg donation due to the very complex, sometimes contradictory, cultural, societal, religious, and legal elements that influence the practice of assisted reproduction.

The Embryo Carrying Agreements Law was, and still is, innovative as regards to providing couples with the very possibility of using surrogacy—even commercial surrogacy—for reproduction. Some Western countries deny this right in its entirety; others limit it to altruistic surrogacy. Similarly, the Egg Donation Law provides couples with the possibility of using ART to procreate by receiving egg donation, including, as mentioned above, the option to combine egg donation and surrogacy. In addition, as part of regulating the procedures of egg donation, the law specifies a fixed compensation that would be paid by the state to the donor.[12]

The Israeli law, in this respect, expands the legitimacy of the use of surrogacy and egg donation. As was mentioned above, several factors underlie this tendency towards expansion. But whatever the explicit or hidden motivations of this phenomenon, the end result is recognition of a relatively wide right to procreate.

But there are limitations. The law's limitation of the use of assisted reproduction may be divided into three elements: (1) preserving a traditional, heterosexual family structure; (2) ensuring some genetic connection to the

---

11 *See* Embryo Carrying Agreements Law; Egg Donation Law. The Egg Donation Law was legislated in 2010. The Embryo Carrying Agreements Law was legislated in 1996 and amended in 2010. Both are subject to amendment proposals and to court appeals, as will be discussed *infra*.

12 Egg Donation Law, section 43.

intended parents; and (3) protecting religious interests. These limitations influence the right to procreate in Israeli law, as will now be discussed.

A Preserving the Traditional, Heterosexual Family Structure

Israeli law is open to assisted reproduction. But, at the same time, it is oriented towards traditional, heterosexual families, while homosexual families or single men and women cannot use some of the assisted reproduction procedures. The Embryo Carrying Agreements Law unequivocally defines intended parents as: "a man and a woman who are a couple, and who contract with a carrying mother for the purpose of giving birth to a child."[13] Thus, a homosexual couple, as well as single men, cannot contract with a woman in a surrogacy agreement.

It should be noted that other, less complex, assisted reproduction technologies are different in this respect. Single women can conceive using an anonymous sperm donation.[14] Accordingly, a lesbian couple can have children using sperm donations without limitations. Both would be considered mothers: one by giving birth to the child; the other, following a judicial decree that declares her to be a second mother of the child.[15] Indeed, if the couple were to separate, the court would be favorably inclined towards the genetic mother, but even here, there are initial signs of change: positions that recognize the rights of the functional, nonbiological, mother as regards her children in cases of separation (especially when the couple has a few children, some of whom are the biological children of the first, and others—of the second, and all are siblings of each other).[16] Lesbian couples accordingly may establish a nuclear family using ART, and would be recognized as such by the law, as opposed to male homosexual couples. The latter cannot reproduce in Israel using ART, but rather are required to use international surrogacy if they wish to procreate.[17]

---

13 Embryo Carrying Agreements Law, section 1.

14 *See* THE PUBLIC COMMISSION FOR THE EVALUATION OF FERTILITY & CHILDBIRTH 33 (2012, Hebrew version available at: http://www.health.gov.il/publicationsfiles/bap2012.pdf) (*henceforth*: Mor-Yosef Commission) (Heb.). The focus of the commission was the possibility of non-anonymous sperm donation (*id.*, at 34–36).

15 *See*, e.g., Family Court File 52940-06-16 G.D. and D.P. v. Attorney General (May 22, 2017) (Heb.) (Isr.).

16 *See* the obiter dictum by Justice Fogelman in Family Appeal Request 4890/14 Plonit v. Plonit (September 2, 2014) (Heb.) (Isr.), section 7: "We cannot say that we cannot recognize joint custody by the members of the same sex of children who were born within the context of this joint relationship."

17 For the problematic aspects of international surrogacy and proposed solutions, *see* Yehezkel Margalit, *From Baby M to Baby M(anji): Regulating International Surrogacy Agreements*, 24 J.L. & POL'Y 41, 87–89 (2015).

Egg donation in this respect is closer to sperm donation, and it may be done even by a single woman. Accordingly, this procedure is relevant for lesbian couples, in which each partner can undergo this process. When the ova are transplanted into the intended mother, the Egg Donation Law lists a number of conditions for approving the process, but these conditions are meant to prevent family connections between the genetic father and the genetic mother and to protect religious interests (see below). The law does not demand that the intended mother or father will be part of a formal, traditional family.[18] Therefore, a single woman (or a woman who belongs to a lesbian family unit) may conceive using an egg which was donated and fertilized by the intended father or by an anonymous sperm donation (that is, in the latter, not necessarily with a genetic connection to either one of the spouses).

The picture is different when the ova are transplanted into a surrogate mother. Here the Egg Donation Law subjects itself to the regulations of the Embryo Carrying Agreements Law, and thereby applies more restrictive rules.[19] Accordingly, again, single women who cannot become pregnant (and surely not male homosexual couples) are prevented from using assisted reproduction, when surrogacy is part of the process.

The result is quite odd: the law de facto recognizes the right of single women and lesbian couples to procreate using sperm or egg donation, but does not provide a similar right for them or for male homosexual couples to procreate using surrogacy. While for single women or lesbian couples procreation is limited only in rare cases (since in most cases they can conceive using sperm donation, and surrogacy is not required) and therefore less significant, for male homosexual couples this prevents their only way to procreate. Whether this is due to historical reasons (the Embryo Carrying Agreements Law was enacted more than 20 years ago, which is a relatively long time, considering the dramatic changes in the family and in family perspectives in recent years, including the status of same-sex couples), or a result of an intentional policy (limiting the right of male homosexual couples to procreate out of religious considerations or because of conservative approaches), this situation can hardly be justified.

Indeed, the Israeli High Court of Justice (*henceforth*: HCJ) sees this situation as discriminating against homosexual couples. In an obiter dictum, the HCJ explains why it seems to be discriminatory legislation. As Justice Jubran writes:

> I find it difficult to accept the situation in which singles and same-sex couples are prevented from realizing their right to become parents by

18 *See* Egg Donation Law, section 13(c)(e)(3).

19 *See* sections 6(b), 11, and 13(a) of the Egg Donation Law.

> contracting surrogacy agreements, while this right is afforded to their heterosexual brothers and sisters. A legal arrangement that imparts a right of legal standing to one group, while barring it from another group due to its identity, preferences, tendencies, or lifestyle, is one seen as discriminatory, which can hardly be deemed proper. I myself find no justification for preferring heterosexual parentage to same-sex parentage in general, and especially as regards realizing the right to be a parent, with the range of techniques for its realization.[20]

The HCJ nevertheless did not as yet change this situation, because of a proposed amendment to the Embryo Carrying Agreements Law which was submitted to the Knesset (the Israeli Parliament) and which passed its first vote (on July 17, 2017, a couple of weeks before the HCJ issued its decision, on August 3, 2017). The HCJ gave the legislator 6 months to complete the amendment legislation process before subjecting it to judicial review. As Chief Justice Naor writes:

> In the final analysis, although the permission to contract surrogacy agreements is not simple, it would seem that that there is no difference between single males or male couples to justify discrimination. To emphasize this once again, this does not establish any rule in these issues. These are merely suppositions. Obviously, the legislator who has these issues before him will have to say his word. To the extent that the legislative processes in the Knesset will not be completed within a reasonable time, the issue will return to this Court, which will discuss it and decide as it sees fit.[21]

It should be noted that the proposed legislation, as of July 2017, does indeed expand the right to surrogacy, but only to single women (and, by implication, to lesbian couples when neither of the spouses can become pregnant). Male homosexual couples, accordingly, would still not be provided with the right to use surrogacy even if the amendment were to be accepted. The probability that the High Court of Justice, on the basis of the above statements, would expand the right to surrogacy to male homosexual couples (either by an activist interpretation of the term "couple" or by striking down the Embryo Carrying Agreement Law as unconstitutional) seems to be quite high.

---

20 HCJ 781/15 Itay Arad-Pinkas, Yoav Arad-Pinkas et al. v. The Surrogacy Agreements Approval Committee and the Knesset (August 3, 2017) (Heb.) (Isr.), Justice Jubran's opinion, section 46.

21 HCJ 781/15 (*supra*, note 20), Chief Justice Naor's opinion, section 6.

As of December 2017, however, the differences between surrogacy and other ARTs still exist: while sperm or egg donation are legally available to a wide spectrum of families, including single parents and lesbian couples, surrogacy is limited to traditional heterosexual couples.

B The Centrality of Genetic Connections

In addition to preserving the classic family structure, the Embryo Carrying Agreements Law requires a genetic tie between the intended parents and the child that will be born. Accordingly, the intended father *must* be the genetic father, while the surrogate mother *need not* be the genetic mother (i.e., full surrogacy, in which the surrogate mother is both the egg owner and gestational mother, is prohibited).[22] The intended mother *may be* the genetic mother, but this is not necessary, and the fertilized ovum may belong to an egg donor, as long as the intended father is the genetic father.[23] Single women cannot go through a process of surrogacy, as discussed in the previous section, but single women can receive an egg donation and conceive using sperm donation. In this case there is no intended father, and the mother—the egg donation receiver—is not the genetic mother, but the fact that she is the carrying mother (or: the physical mother) is sufficient for the purposes of the law. The apparent discrimination against single mothers as regards surrogacy was discussed above, but, according to the proposed amendment to the law, this situation will probably be changed. The demand for genetic ties, however, is a different story.

The High Court of Justice reviewed the demand for genetic ties in surrogacy, and ruled that it is constitutional.[24] According to the court, there are three relevant ties between the child and the parent in surrogacy: the genetic tie (if the intended mother is the egg owner), the physiological tie (the surrogate mother, whose status will be discussed *infra*), and the spousal connection of the intended mother to the father, who has genetic ties to the child (as in a case of surrogacy which includes egg donation, and requires that the intended father will be the sperm owner).[25] The genetic tie (to the father or to both parents), therefore, is a crucial element that validates the carrying agreement, which will lead to declaring the child as the intended parents' child.[26]

22 *See* Embryo Carrying Agreements Law, section 2(d).

23 *See* Egg Donation Law, sections 6(b), 11, and 13.

24 *See* HCJ 781/15 (*supra*, note 20), Justice Jubran's opinion, sections 22–44.

25 Jubran, *id*, based on Justice Hendel's opinion in Family Appeal Request 1118/14 Plonit v. Ministry of Social Affairs and Social Services (April 1, 2015) (Heb.) (Isr.).

26 *Id.*; HCJ 781/15 (*supra*, note 20), Justice Jubran's opinion, section 24.

This requirement, according to the HCJ, accords with the object of the Embryo Carrying Agreement Law, which is to provide a limited and supervised option of using surrogacy, together with ensuring the safety of the gestational mother.[27]

This is not to say that Israeli law does not provide singles or couples who can have neither genetic nor physiological ties to the child with the right to become a parent. This right has already been recognized in Israeli law as a human right, which ensues from a wide set of rights: the right to family, the right to autonomy, the right to privacy, and more.[28] Limiting surrogacy, according to the Israeli Supreme Court, does not violate this right, but rather directs the ways of its fulfillment; therefore, those who lack these ties can become parents in alternative ways, such as adoption or parenthood agreements.[29] The demand for genetic ties in surrogacy is thus a relevant demand, and therefore constitutional, as opposed to the distinction between heterosexual and homosexual couples, which was described by the Court as discriminatory (but the Court decided to wait a few months, for the amendment of the law by the legislator, as discussed above).

From a conceptual viewpoint, genetic parent-child connection, accordingly, has superiority in Israeli law. This, however, does not mean that the law does not recognize alternative parent-child relations. Quite the opposite. Israeli law treats equally various parent-child connections, not only genetic-biological ones. The classic example is, of course, adoption, and other newer ties, such as parenthood by agreement, can be added as well.[30] The outcome, from a conceptual viewpoint, is that the law recognizes alternative parent-child relations, including functional parenthood, psychological parenthood, and other types.[31]

To return to the issue at hand, despite the recognition in Israeli law of alternative parenthood paths, due to the need to limit surrogacy, the Court accepted the argument that surrogacy should be limited to cases in which there is a genetic tie to at least one of the intended parents, while when such ties do not exist, parenthood would be fulfilled using adoption or other parenthood

27 *Id.*, section 39.

28 *See*, e.g., CFH 2401/95 Nahmani v. Nahmani et al. (September 12, 1996) (Isr.) (http://elyon1.court.gov.il/Files_ENG/95/010/024/z01/95024010.z01.HTM; accessed October 16, 2017), section 2 of Chief Justice Barak's dissenting opinion: "From the constitutional viewpoint, of course, we recognize the constitutional liberty to be a parent or not to be a parent. This liberty derives from human dignity and the right to privacy."

29 HCJ 781/15 (*supra*, note 20), Justice Jubran's opinion, section 43.

30 On different types of parenthood and their financial implications, *see*, e.g., Ayelet Blecher-Prigat, *From Partnership to Joint-Parenthood: The Financial Implications of the Joint Parenthood Relationship*, 19 LAW AND BUSINESS—IDC L. REV. 821 (2016).

31 For further conceptual discussion, *see infra*, Part 4.

routes recognized by law. In this respect, it is reasonable to assume that the demand for a genetic tie in surrogacy will not be changed in the near future, as opposed to the limitations that seek to preserve the traditional heterosexual family discussed above.

C Protecting Religious Interests

Jewish law influences Israeli civil law. This is not an innovative statement; we see this in many aspects related to family law. In core marriage and divorce matters religious law is the binding law in Israel.[32] In those matters (although not in all aspects—monetary matters are adjudicated according to civil law [that is applicable to all], rather than personal law) religious law is the positive source of law. The religious affiliation of Israeli civilians, thus, is highly important in determining the law in family matters and personal status issues.[33]

In other aspects of Israeli law, the law is basically civil, but from time to time the legislator takes into account, in varying degree, the position of religious law. For example, outside of family law, Israeli law defines death as brain death for the purpose of organ donation.[34] The law was legislated after consultation with and with the agreement of several Jewish law authorities (although others dispute it) so that religious persons would be able to participate in the highly important project of organ donation.[35]

It is not surprising that the regulation of assisted reproduction takes religious law into consideration due to its centrality in family matters. Both the Embryo Carrying Agreements Law and the Egg Donation Law subject the use of surrogacy and egg donation to various religious considerations. These considerations affect three major areas: parenthood definitions, which will be discussed *infra*,[36] and two realms of restrictions and limitations: limiting participation in surrogacy and egg donation processes to those of the same religious affiliation, and the imposition of restrictions on the participation of married women as egg donors or surrogate mothers.

---

32 *See* Rabbinical Courts Jurisdiction Law (Marriage and Divorce), 5713–1953, sections 1–2.

33 This arrangement is, in fact, an extension of the status quo that existed in British Mandate Palestine, which itself evolved from the Ottoman Empire's Millet legal codes, dating back to the nineteenth century. Despite significant calls for change, and the important process of change brought about by judicial activism, it basically is still binding today. *See* Westreich and Shifman, *supra*, note 10.

34 *See* section 2 of the Brain-Respiratory Death Law, 5768–2008.

35 On the definition of the moment of death and the debate concerning brain death, *see* Avraham Steinberg & Fred Rosner, ENCYCLOPEDIA OF JEWISH MEDICAL ETHICS, 695–711 (2003).

36 *See infra*, Part 4.

The Embryo Carrying Agreements Law requires that the surrogate mother will belong to the same religion as the intended mother, but in the case of non-Jewish mothers, this clause can be disregarded, with the consent of the religious representative in the surrogacy approval committee.[37] Similarly, the Egg Donation Law requires that both donor and recipient will belong to the same religion. The Egg Donation Law does not include the exception of non-Jewish mothers. On the other hand, it does provide "after the fact" legitimacy to by-pass it: in the case of a donor whose religious affiliation is different than the intended mother (either Jewish or non-Jewish), if the ova were already taken, the physician in charge should inform the intended parents of the difference in religious affiliation, and receive their written agreement for the process.[38]

Another restriction on surrogacy and egg donation, which is probably motivated by religious considerations, is the demand that the donor or surrogate mother will be unmarried. The religious aspect of this demand is the fear of declaring the child as a *mamzer* (frequently translated as bastard). When a married woman commits adultery (as well for some other forbidden unions) the born child might be declared a *mamzer*.[39] Declaring a child a *mamzer* has severe consequences: the *mamzer* is prohibited from marrying a Jewish spouse, although the *mamzer* has other legal, financial, and social rights, such as the right to inherit from his parents. Accordingly, a married woman's involvement in a process of reproducing a child not from her husband might, from a religious perspective, be considered the equivalent of extramarital relations, and the child might be considered a *mamzer*. Although some prominent Jewish law decisors reject this view, since according to them one is declared a *mamzer* only when the child was born as a result of a forbidden sexual act, while in surrogacy and egg donation the child was born without the commission of adultery (i.e., without a sexual relationship between the surrogate mother and the father),[40] others do indeed take the stringent view.[41] Accordingly, the fear of

---

37 Embryo Carrying Agreements Law, section 2(5).

38 Egg Donation Law, section 13(e)(3)(a); 13(e)(4).

39 *See* Maimonides, MISHNEH TORAH, *Issurei Bi'ah* (Forbidden Sexual Relations) 15:1.

40 *See* Rabbi SHALOM MORDECHAI SCHWADRON, RESPONSA MAHARSHAM, 3:268 (1962); Rabbi MOSHE FEINSTEIN, RESPONSA IGGROT MOSHE, *Even Ha-'ezer* 1:10 (1959).

41 In the case of sperm donation to a married woman from a man other than her husband, some decisors *see* it as similar to forbidden relationships, including the possible declaration of the child as a *mamzer*, despite the fact that the wife did not actually commit adultery (as opposed to the lenient approach mentioned above). *See*, e.g., Rabbi ITSHAK Y. WEISS, RESPONSA MINHAT ITSHAK, 4:5 (1993). In our cases as well, this stringent opinion might consider the child a *mamzer* due to the participation of a married woman in the process of giving birth to a child from other than her husband.

declaring the child a *mamzer* still exists, and—in order to prevent any possible doubt regarding the proper halakhic status of the child—probably underlies the restrictions on the participation of married women as egg donors or surrogate mothers.

The restrictions on the participation of a married surrogate mother or egg donor are, however, not absolute, and the law permits it in certain cases. The Embryo Carrying Agreements Law requires that the surrogate mother will be unmarried, but permits the participation of a married surrogate mother if, in the opinion of the approval committee, the intended parents could not, with reasonable effort, find an unmarried surrogate mother.[42] The Egg Donation Law bypasses the requirement for an unmarried donor in a slightly different way (similar to an interfaith egg donation): if the ova were already taken, the responsible physician should inform the intended parents that the donor is married, and receive their written agreement for the process.[43]

As a matter of fact, the enforcement of these restrictions has lessened in recent years, especially as regards surrogacy. This is so, in my opinion, because of the wide acceptance of the lenient view that does not declare a child to be a *mamzer* even if the child was born by means of ARTs with the participation of a married woman, since, as mentioned above, no actual adultery was committed with her participation.

Another significant permissive step in this direction was taken as a result of a conceptual development, following a dramatic decision by the former Israeli Chief Rabbi, Shlomo Amar. In 2006 Rabbi Amar permitted a couple that was childless after thirteen years of marriage to enter into a surrogacy agreement with a married surrogate mother.[44] This decision is highly innovative, first, because of the explicit and public permission by a prominent halakhic decisor to use surrogacy,[45] and second, more importantly, because it overcame the traditional fear of involving a third-party married woman in other family relationships, which, as discussed above, might lead to declaring the child a *mamzer*. Rabbi Amar, after consultation with Rabbi Ovadiah Yosef,[46] ruled

42 Embryo Carrying Agreements Law, section 2(3)(a).

43 Egg Donation Law, section 13(e)(4).

44 The case and the Chief Rabbi's approval aroused great interest, and were widely reported in the media. *See*, e.g., Haim Levinson, *Chief Rabbi: Married Woman Can Be Surrogate* (June 11, 2006, http://www.ynetnews.com/articles/0,7340, L-3261249,00.html; accessed October 16, 2017).

45 Many Jewish law decisors object to it; *see infra*, Part 3.

46 Rabbi Ovadiah Yosef (died 2013) is deemed the most prominent and leading Jewish law decisor at the turn of the twenty-first century, especially (but not exclusively) for Sephardic Jewry.

that the genetic mother is considered—without doubt—the child's mother. Therefore, a married surrogate mother can participate in the process, and her connections to the child would not be considered motherhood from the Jewish law perspective.

Rabbi Amar emphasized that this is permitted only when other options are not possible, as in this specific case, but the effect of his decision was nevertheless significant and influential. The Knesset Labor, Welfare and Health Committee discussed the case, and, following Rabbi Amar's decision, the committee called upon the Ministry of Health Board for Approval of Surrogacy Agreements to permit (in exceptional cases) surrogacy agreements with a married surrogate mother.[47] The legal and social reality is developing in this direction, and in recent years the participation of married surrogate mothers has become more common, probably because of the influence of that decision and the recommendation of the Knesset Committee.[48]

These issues, as we already noticed, are very dynamic. These matters, especially the restrictions on assisted reproduction (despite the relative openness of the Israeli system), are continually subject to new challenges and internal change (such as the participation of married women in surrogacy). In addition to repeated appeals to the HCJ (some of them were mentioned above), quite a few public commissions have examined the issue. The last one, the Mor-Yosef Commission, seems to be the most comprehensive and with the greatest potential for influencing the law. Its recommendations, as they pertain to the current discussion, will be discussed in the closing section of this part.

III *Proposals for Changing the Current Legal Situation*

The entire issue of assisted reproduction in Israel was examined by a public commission, which submitted its recommendations in May 2012 (the Mor-Yosef Commission). The commission proposed significant changes in the law, including, as regards surrogacy, permitting altruistic surrogacy in Israel for singles or same-sex couples rather than only for heterosexual couples, as is the case under the current law, while retaining the option of commercial surrogacy for married heterosexual couples.[49] Those recommendations have not (yet) been translated into legislation, but it is to be expected that they will

47 August 18, 2006 (http://www.knesset.gov.il/protocols/data/rtf/avoda/2006-08-15-01.rtf; accessed October 16, 2017) (Heb.).

48 This is attested by one of the approval committee members, Rabbi Yuval Cherlow. *See* Rabbi Elyashiv Knohl, *Halakhic Positions on Surrogacy* (2016), http://www.tzohar.org.il/?p=7352 (Heb.).

49 *See* Mor-Yosef Commission, at 51–65.

be taken into consideration. The HCJ, when it indicated the proper direction and its expectations from the legislator (as discussed above) mentioned *inter alia* the recommendation of this commission.[50] Accordingly, it is reasonable to assume that future amendments to the law will follow these recommendations to some extent: the legislation might provide same sex-couples with the right to use surrogacy in Israel (and thereby would prevent the law from being struck down as unconstitutional), but would maintain some advantage for heterosexual couples, in that only they would be able to use commercial surrogacy.

Were this recommendation to be accepted, it might be challenged in court, due to its apparent discrimination between homosexual and heterosexual couples. The commission, however, justified this difference with two arguments: first, an ethical consideration. Surrogacy uses another woman's body for the need of a third party. The number of heterosexual couples that need surrogacy is relatively small, as opposed to male homosexual couples, for whom surrogacy is the only way to have their (genetic) child. Opening commercial surrogacy to homosexual couples would significantly raise the number of surrogacies in Israel, and might negatively affect the status of women, including the wide commercial "use" of women and objectification of women's bodies. This effect is less dramatic in the current situation, when paid surrogacy is permitted solely for heterosexual couples and the number of surrogacies is relatively small. The second and related argument is based on the object of the law. The law was intended to assist in cases of medical problems that prevent procreation, rather than being the first and main path for procreation. Opening surrogacy to homosexual couples would change this object, and the so greatly increased demand would lessen the possibilities to use surrogacy for procreation by those who were the object of the law in the first place.[51] Indeed, there are counterarguments against this rationale. Yet, it is reasonable that the HCJ would *not* consider the law based on these recommendations as unconstitutional. This is so because, according to these recommendations, the difference between homosexual couples (altruistic surrogacy) and heterosexual couples (both altruistic and commercial surrogacy) does not violate the very right of homosexual couples to procreate using surrogacy, while the difference that does exist is required to ensure the interest of heterosexual couples that cannot reproduce naturally.

As regards genetic ties, the commission did not change the basic requirement for genetic connection in assisted procreation. As mentioned above, that was recognized and approved by the HCJ, because it does not violate the basic

50 HCJ 781/15 (*supra*, note 20), Justice Jubran's opinion, section 39.

51 *See* Mor-Yosef Commission, at 57.

right to become a parent but rather limits one among a number of ways for the fulfillment of this right. The commission recommended expanding the permissibility of egg donation to include already fertilized ova (for example, the remaining fertilized ova of couples who underwent IVF), which, according to the current law, are not explicitly permitted. The commission, however, recommended that since in the case of donated fertilized ova there is no genetic tie to either of the intended parents, it should not be combined with surrogacy. Rather, in such a situation the intended mother must be also the physical mother (who carries and gives birth to the child), so that physical connection to the child would substitute the need for genetic ties.[52]

Another realm that influences the current law's limitations on assisted reproduction, as discussed above, consists of religious considerations as regards the religious affiliation of the participants and as regards restricting the involvement of married women as surrogate mothers and egg donors. This aspect was also examined by the Mor-Yosef Commission. The commission recommended permitting married women to be surrogate mothers.[53] As discussed above, some important Jewish law decisors mitigated the objection to the participation of married women, and notably, former Chief Rabbi Shlomo Amar unhesitatingly approved their inclusion (in certain cases). The recommendations of the commission in this respect continue this trend, and thus would probably be accepted by the legislator. As to the second aspect of the religious limitations discussed above, the commission did not recommend changing the restrictions on interfaith surrogacy or egg donation, probably due to the religious sensitivity of the issue, and since the law itself provides some ways to circumvent this demand.

In conclusion, the Israeli legal system widely recognizes the right to procreate. Yet, despite the relative openness of the Israeli legal system to assisted reproduction, there are significant restrictions due to the traditionality of the society, the desire to guard the interests of couples who cannot procreate due to medical problems, preventing the commodification of women's bodies, and the need to take religious considerations into account. Some of these restrictions are repeatedly challenged in the civil judicial system (such as the distinction between heterosexual and homosexual couples); some are changed as part of internal legal, religious, and social processes; and others are subject to proposals for modifications. Additional changes are in store for us.

---

52 *Id.*, at 40.

53 *Id.*, at 62–64.

Part 2 The Right to Posthumous Fertilization

I *Background*

Two tragic cases have been in the forefront of the Israeli public discussion of posthumous fertilization in recent years. Both involved soldiers who died childless during their military service. Death, and especially that of young persons, naturally arouses strong emotions which influence the discussion of posthumous fertilization. In the Israeli context, however, when such a process involves dead soldiers, the entire discussion is much more charged and complicated. The sensitivity of Israeli society to the death of soldiers is influenced by a sense of shared responsibility, the marked respect shown for the ultimate sacrifice made for the state, and the perception of this act as (civil) martyrdom. The desire of the family (especially the soldier's parents) to act in the name of their son, to bring some relief to their mourning, and to provide continuity for the deceased soldier is very intense, and public support for and solidarity with these bereaved families is extremely high.

In the Shahar case, for example, the parents complained that the state obligates them to send their child to the battlefield, but they become "meaningless," and they lose their status as parents together with the loss of their son.[1] This argument emphasizes the expectations of the parents for national, public, and legal support, and the acceptance of their request, along with society's duty to assist in giving them closure. The Shahar and Shaked cases accordingly were much more complex and emotional than other (also very sensitive) cases, with the intensive involvement of the Israeli public, media, legislators, and the courts.

But even without these special considerations, posthumous fertilization poses difficult dilemmas and raises conflicts concerning the right to procreate and the wish for continuity, on the one hand, and, on the other, social and policy considerations in favor of restricting the use of this technique. The major considerations of this sort are the social consequences of bringing children lacking at least one parent into the world, the psychological effect of being born as a living memory, together with philosophical and theological concerns regarding human intervention in life after death.[2]

1 *See* Family Appeal Request 7141/15 Plonit v. Plonit et al. (December 22, 2016) (Heb.) (Isr.), section 21 of Justice Hayut's opinion.

2 For a critical analysis of the support of postmortem sperm retrieval, *see* Hashiloni-Dolev and Triger, *infra*, note 19. Needless to say, in addition to the specific difficulties inherent in these technologies, the general criticism of the increased use of ART might be applied here as well. *See*, e.g., regarding the trend of preferring ART over adoption: Bartholet, *supra*, Part 1 note 7.

Israel is quite open to ART, as discussed above, and posthumous fertilization is no different. Some countries forbid posthumous fertilization entirely. Others permit it in a very limited way. In some countries posthumous fertilization is not regulated by state legislation, but the use of this technology is rather based on public policies.[3] In Israel, the subject was regulated until recently on the basis of the Attorney General Guidelines (October 2003) and was inspired by the recommendations of a few commissions, including the latest one (the Mor-Yosef Commission), which have not (yet) been transformed into legislation, but were published and explicitly or implicitly influence the public discourse.[4] In December 2016 the Israeli Supreme Court issued its decision in the case of Shaked Meiri (one of the above-mentioned soldiers' cases), and thereby delineated the obligatory principles in this matter (although the story has not yet ended, as will be described below). According to the Supreme Court, there is indeed an existing right to procreate that applies also to posthumous fertilization, but with a significant limitation, according to which the spouse of the dead person—and only the spouse—is entitled to decide on implementation.

Before turning to a deeper analysis of the right to posthumous fertilization, I would like to make two remarks. First, in the current legal situation, posthumous fertilization is permitted not only when there is an expressed desire of the deceased, but also when there is a presumed desire of the deceased (although restricted to the decision of the spouse). A few children have been born in Israel by posthumous fertilization, either when the person was ill and made an explicit living will for posthumous sperm retrieval or after a sudden death, on the basis of the presumed desire.[5] The two cases mentioned above are more

---

3 For the background and a survey and comparative discussion of the legal status of posthumous sperm retrieval in the United States, Europe, and Israel, *see* Jon B. Evans, *Post-mortem Semen Retrieval: A Normative Prescription for Legislation in the United States*, 1 CONCORDIA L. REV. 133, 136–153 (2016); Rabbi J. David Bleich, *Survey of Recent Halakhic Periodical Literature: Posthumous Paternity* 49 TRADITION 72, 73–76 (2016). For a preliminary comparison between Israel and a few other countries, *see* Mor-Yosef Commission at 45 note 15.

4 *See* Mor-Yosef Commission, at 43–50.

5 The concept of "biological will" (representing a living will of posthumous sperm retrieval) was conceived and developed by the Israeli New Family organization, and was used and approved in a few cases. *See* http://www.newfamily.org.il/en/biological-will-precedents-2/ (accessed October 15, 2017). Anecdotally, in an exceptional case an Israeli family court recognized posthumous adoption. In that case, the spouses were foster parents of a child, and went through the process of adoption, but the mother passed away from cancer before its completion. The Beersheva Family Court ruled that, due to the unique circumstances of the case (including the parent-child relationships that had developed between the child and the couple), the adoption decree would be

complex, since they also entailed internal family conflicts and other considerations, which challenged the basic attitude towards posthumous fertilization. Through their analysis in the next section we will seek to clarify the attitude of Israeli law and Israeli society on this issue.

Second, the Supreme Court in the Shaked Meiri case did not discuss the use of frozen ova of a deceased woman. The case dealt only with posthumous sperm retrieval. Nevertheless, despite the differences in the complexity of the process between posthumous sperm retrieval and the posthumous use of ova,[6] if a woman expresses before she dies her wish to procreate, or her spouse wishes to provide continuity for her, there is no reason to differentiate between the cases.[7]

II *The Parents' Right to Posthumous Fertilization*

Shaked Meiri was a reserve soldier who died during a military exercise when he was 27 years old (September 2004). Meiri wed only three months prior to his death and was childless, which made his death that much more tragic. Following the recommendation of army officials, and with the agreement of his widow (who later changed her mind) and the active support of his parents, his sperm was extracted and frozen. Had the widow agreed to continue with the process and be inseminated from his sperm, that probably would have been approved by the court on the basis of the Attorney General's Guidelines. But she objected, remarried, and had her own children from the new relationship. His parents requested to use his sperm to impregnate another woman (either as an anonymous sperm donation or to a woman who would agree to raise the child of the deceased), and their request was approved by the family court. The widow's appeal to the district court was rejected, and the case came before the Supreme Court.[8]

retroactively valid, from a time that preceded the mother's death, who posthumously became an adoptive parent. *See* Adoption File 22-17 *Plonit and Ploni vs. Attorney General* (September 13, 2017), PsakDin Legal Database (Heb.), available at https://www.psakdin.co.il/Court/1464692#.WgXYKdJBoYo (accessed November 10, 2017).

6 Unfertilized ova require an IVF process with a surrogate (or intended) mother. Fertilized ova require only placing in the uterus of the surrogate or intended mother. Both (the latter, and surely the former) are more complex procedures compared to artificial insemination, which is necessary in posthumous sperm retrieval.

7 This is also the recommendation of the Mor-Yosef Commission, at 49–50.

8 For the details of the case, *see* Family Appeal Request 7141/15 Plonit v. Plonit et al. (December 22, 2016) (Heb.) (Isr.), sections 1–6 of Justice Hayut's opinion. For a media report, *see*, e.g., Jeremy Sharon, "Supreme Court Prevents Use of Dead Soldier's Sperm,"

In a lengthy and reasoned verdict, the Supreme Court denied the right of the parents to decide regarding the use of their dead child's sperm and gave his widow the exclusive right to make such a decision. The court reasoned that parents should not be involved in their child's decision to procreate, and that this is a private decision of the couple. Since the widow in that case objected to the process, the court ruled that the parents are not allowed to proceed with the use of their son's sperm.[9]

Omri Shahar was a 25-year-old promising career officer when he died in a tragic road accident (June 2012). His sperm was extracted from his body and frozen right after his death, and his parents later appealed to a family court to permit them to have a child from his sperm using an egg donation with a surrogate mother and to raise the child as their own. In a precedent-setting decision, a family court approved their request in September 2016.[10] In February 2017, however, following the Supreme Court's decision in the Meiri case, the District Court reversed this decision, and disallowed the use of Omri Shahar's sperm.

The District Court denied Omri Shahar's parents their right to continue with the procreation process using their son's sperm. The court reasoned that, following the decision in the Meiri case, the right to procreate is reserved exclusively for the spouse. Omri Shahar had a permanent partner, but they did not formally establish their relationship (although they intended to do so). His spouse supported the process, but she did not want to be an active participant. The District Court consequently reasoned that, despite her support, the process could not be performed by the parents.[11] The decision was approved by the Supreme Court, which rejected a request to submit an appeal to the District Court decision, reasoning that the decision in the Meiri case applied

---

http://www.jpost.com/Israel-News/Supreme-Court-prevents-use-of-dead-soldiers-sperm-486082 (April 4, 2017) (accessed October 2, 2017).

9 *See* Family Appeal Request 7141/15 (*supra*, note 8). This is also the position of the Mor-Yosef Commission, at 44–46, and the position of the Sperm Banks Proposed Legislation, 2016, sections 68–74. The Ethics Committee of the Israel Fertility Association (IFA) has recently published its recommendations regarding postmortem sperm retrieval, and, for the most part, adopted a similar position. *See* POSITION PAPER ON THE USE OF SPERM FROM THE DECEASED: THE RECOMMENDATIONS AND CONCLUSIONS OF THE ETHICS COMMITTEE OF THE ISRAEL FERTILITY ASSOCIATION, November 2017.

10 *See* Family Court File 16699-06-13 Shahar v. Attorney General (September 27, 2017) (Heb.) (Isr.).

11 For the District Court's decision, *see* Family Appeal 45930-11-16 The State of Israel v. Shahar (January 27, 2017) (Heb.) (Isr.).

here as well, so that the parents cannot initiate the process of sperm retrieval without the participation of the spouse (even if she agrees to the process).[12]

There are significant differences between the cases, and especially the fact that Shahar did not have a formal spouse, but rather a partner who did not object to the process (although not wanting to participate in it). The District Court, however, with the agreement of the Supreme Court, rejected these differences. The court refused to use a limiting interpretation of the negation of the parents' right to perform sperm retrieval and approve the parents' request, but rather applied here the Meiri ruling in its entirety.

The District Court brought an additional reason, which is related to our discussion in the previous part: Omri Shahar's parents request to use their son's sperm and to raise the child needed the participation of both an egg donor and a surrogate mother. According to the Carrying Agreements Law, however, a genetic tie of one of the intended parents is required in order to approve surrogacy.[13] When the deceased's spouse agrees to the process and will be the intended parent, according to the Attorney General Guidelines and the recommendations of the Mor-Yosef Commission, even if she (in the case of sperm retrieval) does not have any genetic or physical connection to the child (i.e., both an egg donor and a surrogate mother would participate in the fertilization process) the spouse's "tie to the [deceased's genetic] tie" satisfies the law. But in the Shahar case, neither the intended father nor the intended mother (Asher and Irit Shahar, Omri's parents) had this kind of tie, and therefore the process cannot be approved.[14] The court could have used a creative widening interpretation and view the parents as having a sufficient tie, but decided to reject this option: "The Respondents cannot be deemed as having a tie to the tie, and only the partner of the deceased can meet this requirement."[15]

Public acceptance of the two decisions was mixed. The cases are frequently mentioned and debated in the public sphere, with (according to the author's impression) an apparent tendency to acceptance of the parents' demand. The Israeli public is sympathetic to Omri Shahar's parents' claimed right to raise a child from their son's sperm, and feels they are capable of doing so. Shaked Meiri's case is more complex because of the refusal of his widow to the process. Some participants to the debate argue that the widow, who established a new relationship and has children from that relationship, should not be afforded

12 *See* Family Appeal Request 1943/17 Shahar v. The State of Israel (August 15, 2017) (Heb.) (Isr.).

13 *See supra*, Part 1, section II.B.

14 Family Appeal 45930-11-16 (*supra*, note 11), sections 59, 62, 66 of Judge Weitzman's opinion.

15 *Id.*, section 66.

the right to negate continuity for her deceased husband. In general, the parents' demand is viewed very sympathetically in the public discourse.[16]

Leaving aside the harsh results of the above decisions from the parents' personal perspective, it is significant that the Israeli Supreme Court did not deny the right of a person to continuity after his or her death. Quite the opposite, the court did acknowledge that a person has a right to posthumous procreation using the deceased's sperm (or ova). Usually, however, determining the intention of the deceased is difficult (unless he or she explicitly expressed his/her wishes), and the Court (following the Attorney General Guidelines) solely empowered the spouse to make this decision (or: express the deceased's will).

Interestingly, although the Supreme Court accepts (with some limitations) the right to posthumous fertilization, which is, despite its limitations, quite revolutionary comparing to other countries,[17] the decision still reflects an attitude that preserves the traditional family structure. The deceased's spouse is provided with the right to procreate using her or his spouse's gametes, which gives priority to the nuclear traditional family unit. The Supreme Court explained its reliance on the spouse's decision in a different way, reasoning that only the spouse is capable of properly expressing the deceased's will, but, beneath the surface, this expresses the more traditional approach. In this respect, it accords with the basic attitude of Israeli law as regards surrogacy and egg donation, which, despite its openness, still strives to preserve the nuclear traditional family, as discussed in the previous part.[18]

---

16 *See*, e.g., the debate between Prof. Shalom Rosenberg, whose expertise is Jewish philosophy, and Rabbi Yuval Cherlow, who has done extensive work in the field of Jewish ethics, in the SHABBAT weekly magazine of the MAKOR RISHON newspaper: the former unequivocally supports the parents' requests, while the latter hesitates (Shalom Rosenberg, *A Grandchild without a Father*, SHABBAT—MAKOR RISHON, May 5, 2017, http://preview.tinyurl.com/yc7xahfz; Yuval Cherlow, *The Characteristic of Sodom?—Response*, SHABBAT—MAKOR RISHON, May 19, 2017, https://tinyurl.com/y8sf5cqh; Shalom Resenberg, *When a Right Turns Cruel*, SHABBAT—MAKOR RISHON, May 26, 2017, https://tinyurl.com/yanqgqtd; all accessed October 16, 2017) (Heb.). Prof. Assa Kasher, in a dissenting opinion to the recommendations of the Mor-Yosef Commission regarding posthumous fertilization (Mor-Yosef Commission, at 46–48), too, argues that the parents should be provided with the right to decide regarding the procreation of their deceased son, using his sperm. It is noteworthy that Kasher's son was killed in an accident during his military service, which led to almost full solidarity and complete identification with the parents' demand.

17 *See supra*, note 3.

18 *See supra*, Part 1.

There is, to be short, a right to posthumous procreation which is under the control of the deceased's spouse. But this is not the final word on this issue. Proposed legislation was submitted to the Knesset (the Israeli parliament) in June 2017 regarding the right to posthumous sperm retrieval of fallen soldiers.[19] Knesset members from across the political spectrum support entitling the parents of deceased soldiers to use their son's sperm. The explanation appended to the proposed legislation provides the rationale behind the proposal by indicating some unique aspects of deceased soldiers' cases which justify the exceptional arrangement in their case, and especially the justice in providing parents with this right. We mentioned above the public's sensitivity regarding fallen soldiers, its support, and other factors, which are at the basis of the public debate, and are also mentioned in this explanation as the rationale of the proposal. But in my opinion, this is not merely a question related to the special character of these cases. Rather, the proposal reflects a much deeper rationale, which touches upon the very conceptualization of posthumous fertilization. I would like to explore this argument.

III *The Future of the Parents' Right to Posthumous Fertilization: Two Concepts of the Right to Procreation*

A The Supreme Court vs. Proposed Legislation: Two Concepts

The Supreme Court decision in Shaked Meiri's case focused on will—that of the deceased person. Providing his widow with the right to decide was described as a means for revealing his presumed will. His parents' request, supported by public opinion, on the other hand, focused on different kinds of argument: continuity, the parents' feelings, and society's collective responsibility to the soldier and his family. This is emphasized in the explanation of the proposed legislation, which goes in this direction:

> The proposed legislation is meant to regulate the continuity of the soldier who died during his military service and did not leave offspring, by giving his wife, his permanent partner, or his parents the right to take sperm from him after his death and to use it to conceive a child.
>
> The State of Israel, which is experienced in the pain of bereavement, has lost its finest sons and daughters who fell in the defense of the country's security. The lives of young soldiers were cut short in their prime, and the State of Israel owes a moral obligation to the bereaved families who have lost what is most precious to them [...] The responsibility of the

19 Fallen Soldier's Sperm Retrieval Law. The proposal was submitted as an amendment to the Fallen Soldiers' Families Law (Pensions and Rehabilitation) 5710–1950, section 35b.

> State that sends its sons to defend its security [...] must be expressed also in affording the possibility of making use of advanced technologies that will enable the bereaved families to have offspring from the deceased and to maintain [the dead soldier's] continuity.

These two sources—the court and the proposal—reflect different kinds of argumentations, or: two types of conceptualizations of the right to posthumous fertilization. The first focuses on the will of the deceased individual. I would define this conceptualization as an *individualistic right to reproduce* posthumously. The second focuses on family continuity, feelings of responsibility, and the need to compensate the families. I would define it as a *familial right to reproduce* posthumously.[20]

Defining the argumentations as individualistic vs. familial (or, in a wider definition, communal) views them as two different ideal types. In reality, however, they are intermingled (i.e., we can find traces of the familial arguments in the Supreme Court decision, and traces of an individualistic approach in the proposed legislation). The issue, however, is dominancy. And here, we view a fascinating move from the individualistic argument to the communal one. The Supreme Court focused on individualistic arguments. This enabled the court to exclude the parents from the right to decide regarding their deceased child's procreation. The proposed legislation focuses on familial and communal argumentations, and therefore provides the parents with this right.

An interesting point in this respect is that the proposed legislation does not intend to adopt this argumentation for all cases of posthumous fertilization, but rather to limit it to fallen soldiers. Thus, it accepts that individualistic argumentations are at the center of the discussion, but makes an exception.[21]

---

20 A different analysis of the current legal situation is proposed by Yael Hashiloni-Dolev and Zvi Triger. Hashiloni-Dolev and Triger use a critical approach to argue that the current legal discourse which focuses on revealing the "will" of the deceased is based on patriarchal views and pronatalism. They argue, accordingly, that the discourse should shift to discussing the right of the spouse and the presumed agreement of the deceased. *See* Yael Hashiloni-Dolev & Zvi Triger, *Between the Deceased's Wish and the Wishes of His Surviving Relatives: Posthumous Children, Patriarchy, Pronatalism, and the Myth of Continuity of the Seed*, 39 IYUNEI MISHPAT (TAU L. REV.) 661 (2016). My argument here differs in two aspects. First, it uses a functionalist approach to analyze the current legal discourse, and therefore focuses on the rationale behind the current arguments within the rights discourse. Second, it suggests an internal distinction within the rights discourse, between individualistic and communal right.

21 For cases other than fallen soldiers, the Supreme Court decision, the Attorney General Guidelines, the recommendation of the Mor-Yosef Commission, and the Sperm Banks

In the case of fallen soldiers, as mentioned above, due to the sensitivity of the issue and the stormy emotions that it arouses, we see a paradigmatic conceptual change, from one kind of right to another, which makes it possible to provide family members (in addition to the spouse) with the right to initiate posthumous fertilization.

B The Ancient Predecessor of the Two-Concepts Model

The tension between individualistic and familial conceptualization already appears in the ancient Biblical predecessor of the modern posthumous fertilization debate. According to Biblical law, if a married man dies childless his wife should marry his brother in a levirate marriage. If they do not conduct levirate marriage, they should perform the ritual act of *halitzah*, and thereby unbind the tie between the widow and her brother-in-law.[22] Today, most Jewish communities do not practice levirate marriage, but rather engage in *haltizah*.[23] The rationale of levirate marriage law, however, is still relevant—and not surprisingly, is the very rationale of posthumous fertilization.

The Biblical commandment states:

> If brothers dwell together, and one of them dies and has no son, the wife of the dead shall not be married outside the family to a stranger; her husband's brother shall go in to her, and take her as a wife, and perform the duty of a husband's brother to her.
>
> And the first son whom she bears *shall succeed to the name of his brother who is dead*, that his name may not be blotted out of Israel.[24]

The object of the levirate marriage is to "succeed to the name of his brother who is dead." But what does this mean? One possible, literal, interpretation is that the firstborn would be named after the deceased. Alternatively, to "succeed to the name of his brother" might be a form of continuation for the deceased in its broader sense. In a wider Biblical context, that would mean to inherit the land of the dead brother, as in the case of the daughters of Zelophehad son of Hepher who asked to inherit their father (who died without a son):

Law Proposed Legislation (*see supra*, note 9) would still be applicable. There is accordingly no contradiction between the two legislation proposals.

22 *See* Deuteronomy 25: 5–10.

23 *See* Elimelech Westreich, *Levirate Marriage in the State of Israel: Ethnic Encounter and the Challenge of a Jewish State*, 37 Isr. Law Rev. 427 (2003–2004).

24 Deuteronomy 25:5–6 (Revised Standard Version translation).

> Why should *the name of our father* be taken away from his family because he had no son? *Give to us a possession* among our father's brethren.[25]

This seems to be a classic interpretative issue, but it has legal implications. These two options (the textual and the contextual) are already mentioned in the Talmudic literature, which discusses which interpretation should be adopted from a halakhic-legal perspective. The Talmud cites a Tannaitic source, which examines the two interpretations, and concludes:

> "Shall succeed to the name of his brother," in respect of inheritance.
>
> You say: "in respect of inheritance," perhaps it does not [mean that], but "in respect of the name": [if the deceased, for instance, was called] Joseph [the child] shall be called Joseph; if Johanan he shall be called Johanan!—Here it is stated, "shall succeed to the name of his brother" and elsewhere it is stated, "They shall be called after the name of their brethren in their inheritance", as the "name" that was mentioned there [has reference to] inheritance, so the "name" which was mentioned here [also has reference] to inheritance.[26]

The Talmud thus acknowledges the two options as possible interpretations of the Biblical text, but, based on contextual considerations, adopts the contextual one. This Talmudic passage seems to make a clear-cut interpretative decision. In fact, as David Henshke shows, different Talmudic sources adopted the other, local-textual interpretation, that of naming the child after the deceased.[27]

Classic, post-Talmudic, commentators also moved between these two options, such as the eleventh century French commentator Rabbi Shlomo Itzhaki (Rashi), on the one hand, who interprets "name" as inheritance (following the conclusion of the Babylonian Talmud passage, cited above), and the twelfth century French commentator Rabbi Joseph Bekhor Shor, who adds to the Talmudic interpretation that the literal meaning of the text is giving the born child the name of the deceased.[28] Interestingly, another classic commentator of that period, Rabbi Joseph Kra (French, tenth-eleventh centuries) testifies to a custom of Ashkenazic communities that, in practice, adopts the two

---

25 Numbers 27:4 (RSV).

26 Babylonian Talmud, Yevamot 24a.

27 *See* David Henshke, *Two Subjects Typifying the Tannaitic Halakhic Midrash*, 65 TARBIZ 417, 420–427 (1996) (Heb.) For the two options in Josephus, *see* id, at 422 note 19.

28 *See* Rashi, s.v. "*Yakum*" and Bekhor Shor, s.v. "*Yakum*" to Deuteronomy 25:6.

options—the simple meaning of "name" and the contextual meaning (which was adopted by the Talmud): "The Jews in Mainz and Worms practiced that, God forbid, when such a thing happened in their time [that is, a man who died childless and his wife underwent levirate marriage], they require fulfilment [of the commandment by] the actual giving of [the deceased's] name [to the born child], and also by inheritance [of the deceased by his brother,] to fulfil the Soferic [interpretation.]"[29]

The more challenging part of this Biblical passage, however, is the last word of the Hebrew verse: "on the name of his *brother* who is dead"—who comes on the name of whom? If it is the child that would be born from the levirate marriage, this child is not the brother of the deceased person.[30] If it is the brother-in-law who marries the widow in the levirate marriage, the first part of the verse cannot be correctly interpreted, since he is not "the first son whom she bears." The difficulty in interpreting the verse led to the existence of the two interpretations. Apparently, the dominant interpretation in the Talmudic and post-Talmudic sources is the latter, that "his brother" refers to the brother-in-law, who inherits his deceased brother, but there are those who interpret it as referring to the born child; and even the Talmud, which chooses the second interpretation, admits that there are interpretative difficulties in this understanding: "Said Rava: although throughout the Torah no text loses its ordinary meaning, here the gezerah shavah [=an interpretative method of expounding the Biblical text by comparing two separate passages] has come and entirely deprived the text of its ordinary meaning."[31]

Clearly, if we interpret "name" literally (naming), we must interpret "his brother" as the first option, namely, the deceased. We do find child-parent relations that are defined as brotherhood, and this is probably the meaning here.[32] The born child, although biologically the child of the brother-in-law, bears the name of the deceased brother, and is considered his child. According to the other option, levirate marriage is a form of familial continuation. First, it focuses on family possessions: inheritance of the land, which has symbolic and substantive familial importance, especially in an ancient agricultural

29 Rabbi Joseph Kara, Deuteronomy 25:6, s.v. "*Vehayah*." One or two generations later, however, Ashkenazic communities stopped practicing levirate marriage, and made *halitzah* mandatory.

30 Some translations accordingly omit the possessive determiner "his," which is present in the Hebrew text.

31 Babylonian Talmud, Yevamot 24a, and *see* Henshke, *supra*, note 25.

32 *See* Genesis 31:46, in which the Hebrew word *le-ehav* (literally, "unto his brethren," as this is rendered in the King James translation) refers to his sons.

culture. Second, even more clearly, it does not focus on the genealogical (in modern terms: genetic) links to the deceased person, but rather on the wider familial ties: the one who continues the deceased is his brother, who marries his wife and inherits him.[33]

These two related interpretive dilemmas ("name" and "brother") are accordingly significant for understanding the purpose of the laws of levirate marriage. There are two interpretive options of the Biblical text, that fulfil two different objects: personal and familial, and which exist in various layers of interpretation—from the simple meaning of the Biblical text, through Talmudic sources and up to post-Talmudic commentators. Needless to say, on the basis of this analysis, the two objects are close to the two different concepts of posthumous procreation, and might even shed more light on them.

Indeed, in ancient times posthumous sperm retrieval was impossible, but its object—either individualistic or familial—could be achieved (and was encouraged) via levirate marriage. It is not surprising, due to the general openness of Israeli society to assisted reproduction and the important place of procreation within this society, to find this equivalence. In this respect, this ancient predecessor (levirate marriage) can be seen as a cultural inspiration for modern Israeli approaches in favor of posthumous sperm retrieval.[34]

---

33 This interpretation is supported by a wide Biblical context: in addition to the case of the daughters of Zelophehad mentioned above, another case shares a similar view: the marriage of Ruth and Boaz (Ruth 4). The motivation of the characters in this case is quite similar: to provide family continuity by a new family marital relationship. For this and other objectives in the book of Ruth, see Bernard S. Jackson, *Ruth, the Pentateuch and the Nature of Biblical Law: In Conversation with Jean Louis Ska*, 75, 90–91, THE POST-PRIESTLY PENTATEUCH: NEW PERSPECTIVES ON ITS REDACTIONAL DEVELOPMENT AND THEOLOGICAL PROFILES (Konrad Schmid and Federico Giuntoli eds., 2015) The story of Tamar and Judah's family (Genesis 38), on the other hand, supports the first interpretative option. The refusal of Judah's second son, Onan, to impregnate Tamar was because "Onan knew that the offspring would not be his" (Genesis 38:9), that is, his child would be considered the deceased brother's child. Interestingly, according to 1 Chronicles 4:21, the son of Shelah (Judah's third son) was called Er, probably after Shelah's deceased brother, Er (again, following the first interpretative option; my thanks to Avigail Zohar for this reference). It should be noted that both stories are not formal levirate marriages but rather voluntary ones, which emphasizes the strength of the idea of personal and family continuity in the Biblical context.

34 In this context, *see* Ya'arit Bokek-Cohen and Vardit Ravitsky, *Soldiers' Preferences Regarding Sperm Preservation, Posthumous Reproduction, and Attributes of a Potential "Posthumous Mother,"* OMEGA—JOURNAL OF DEATH AND DYING (forthcoming, 2017). Bokek-Cohen and Ravitsky's study examines the view of Israeli soldiers regarding posthumous

Due to the equivalence, it is not surprising also that modern Jewish law decisors are quite open to posthumous fertilization as an individualistic right, as a form of family continuation, or as both.[35] We will now discuss these views.

IV *Posthumous Fertilization: Modern Jewish Law*

Posthumous fertilization is approved by important Jewish law decisors, as well, which aids in its acceptance by the Jewish majority in Israel, and to dispose the legislator and the court to encourage (or at least approve) its use. As we saw above, the boundaries of the right to posthumous fertilization are not always universally recognized in the Israeli discourse, and as is common in this kind of debate, some of the participants in the legal and public discourse use Jewish law (and Jewish ethics) in support of their position, frequently (as regarding the right of the parents to initiate this process), for the expanded use of this practice.[36] Specifically, Jewish law was one of the sources of Justice Melcer's dissenting opinion in the Meiri case, according to which the parents should be provided with the right to decide about retrieving their son's sperm, even when the widow objects.[37]

In the Meiri case, some writers, based on Jewish law, expressed their supportive opinion of the parents' demand, either by formal opinion submitted to the court or in the public sphere.[38] A more authoritative opinion, by a widely recognized halakhic decisor, is that of Rabbi Zalman Nehemya Goldberg. Rabbi Goldberg (born 1932), a former judge (*dayyan*) in the Israeli High Rabbinical

---

fertilization. It finds a relatively high predisposition for posthumous fertilization, and considerable influence of the soldiers' parents on soldiers' willingness for such a process.

35 Similar integration (and sometimes tension) between two very proximate aspects may be found, in my opinion, in classic Jewish law sources on marriage. For example, according to one of the most important codes of Jewish law, *Arba'ah Turim* of R. Jacob ben Asher (Germany and Spain, thirteenth–fourteenth centuries), marriage combines the individualistic desire for partnership ("It is not good that the man should be alone" [Gen. 2:18,]) and procreation (to "be fruitful and multiply" [Genesis 1:28]), which has more of a societal character. *See* Avishalom Westreich, *Book Review: Melanie Landau, Tradition and Equality in Jewish Marriage: Beyond the Sanctification of Subordination* 28 Nashim: A Journal of Jewish Women's Studies and Gender Issues 147, 149 (2015).

36 Intriguingly, in other matters, Jewish law is charged with being restrictive and conservative (e.g., in matters of marriage and divorce). Here, however, it is quite the opposite.

37 *See* Family Appeal Request 7141/15 (*supra*, note 1).

38 Prof. Aviad Hacohen submitted a formal opinion to the Family Court in support of the parents' request, based on Jewish law (Family Court File 16699-06-13, *supra*, note 10). In the public sphere, *see* the debate between Prof. Rosenberg and Rabbi Cherlow, *supra*, note 16.

Court and a well-known halakhic decisor, who is accepted by all sectors of Jewish Orthodoxy in Israel and abroad, explicitly approves the use of posthumous fertilization. Rabbi Goldberg was asked by an official state committee for his position on several reproduction matters. Concerning posthumous sperm retrieval, he replied:

> Without the agreement of the deceased, it is obviously forbidden. But if there is an explicit agreement, or even a clear presumption that this is his will, there is no prohibition in this matter.[39]

Interestingly, Rabbi Goldberg adds a general remark regarding the position of Jewish law on issues of this sort:

> We note that according to Jewish law we need a reason to forbid, and without such a reason the natural situation is to permit. In this regard, relevant also is the fact that the Torah afforded great importance to the human desire to leave a name and remembrance in the world, as we can learn from the laws of levirate marriage.[40]

This remark, as can be concluded from reviewing a wide range of issues regarding assisted reproduction, seems to correctly reflect the attitude of Jewish law on this matter, and to explain the high level of motivation and wide support among Israeli society for ART. Specifically, regarding posthumous sperm retrieval, Goldberg's starting point is that it should not be prohibited. He then adds an important reason, not only for permitting, but also for encouraging this practice: the natural desire for procreation, "to leave a name and remembrance," which was the basis for the laws of levirate marriage (as discussed above).

Following this basic attitude, it is usually agreed that Jewish law permits posthumous fertilization although it is not unanimously accepted.[41] The discussion thus focuses on secondary questions, such as the extent to which the deceased is considered the father of the child: is there a parental relationship

---

39 Zalman N. Goldberg, *On Egg Donation, Surrogacy, Freezing the Sperm of a Single Man, and Extracting Sperm from a Corpse: Response to the Commission for the Approval of Agreements for Carrying Fetuses by Rabbi Zalman Nehemiah Goldberg*, 65–66 ASSIA 45 (1999) (Heb.).

40 *Id.*

41 *See*, e.g., Rabbi Ig'al Shafran, *Posthumous Fatherhood*, 20 TECHUMIN (2000) (Heb.), who strongly objects to this practice.

between them, and if so, does such a relationship exist for every legal aspect (inheritance, exempting the widow from levirate marriage or *halitzah* [since the deceased did not die childless], and the fulfilment of the obligation to "be fruitful and multiply")? As is common in this sort of questions, opinions vary from (very few) who do not see the child as the deceased's child at all, to those who acknowledge parental relationships for several matters (usually, in this group, excluding the exemption from levirate marriage or *halitzah*), and those who see the child as the deceased's child in all respects.[42]

V *Summary*

Israeli law recognizes the right for posthumous fertilization, and, in particular, posthumous sperm retrieval. This recognition accords with the general openness of Israeli law to the use of assisted reproductive technologies, and is supported by public opinion and views within Jewish law (whose impact on Israeli law cannot be exaggerated).

The question of boundaries and balances, however is crucial here. Thus, despite the fundamental recognition of the right to procreate, the legal system had to limit it. The results were difficult: the current boundaries were set in the two tragic cases (Shaked Meiri and Omri Shahar) by providing the deceased's spouse with the exclusive right to decide, and the spouse's decision is assumed to reflect the will of the deceased. An expanded right—that of the parents, either as an alternative way for reflecting the deceased's will, or as independent right holders (the right for family continuation)—was rejected. Indeed, we can still expect dynamism in this matter. Proposed legislation might change this situation, and expand the right to posthumous fertilization to fallen soldiers' parents.

It should be emphasized that the spouse in the current legal situation is not provided with a substantive right to procreate using her or his spouse's gametes. Rather, the spouse is entitled to speak for the deceased. In this way we bridge between death and life, between those who have the right to procreate, and those who can express it. The main focus continues to be the deceased's own will. But even as such, in my opinion, the way might be opened for alternatives—either wider options for reflecting the deceased's will, or a wider right to posthumous procreation. The latter, as discussed in this part, reflects a different conceptualization: familial continuation rather than individualistic procreation. Having made this observation, it is possible, therefore, that we would witness a change in the legal situation in the near future.

---

42 *See* the discussion of Rabbi Bleich: Bleich (*supra*, note 3), at 76–89.

Part 3 Conceptual Implications of the Modern Right to Procreate

I *Background*

We discussed in previous parts two major issues of ART in Israel: the right to procreate (focusing mainly on surrogacy and egg donation) and the right to posthumous fertilization. Our starting points and main focus were the legal-practical levels, which enabled us to examine normative and conceptual dimensions, as regards the right to procreate and the right to posthumous fertilization. The focus of the current part is conceptual: parenthood definitions in Israeli law, as are reflected in current discourse of assisted reproductive technologies.[1]

As an opening remark, I would like to explore a few preliminary insights regarding parenthood definitions and the conceptualization of parenthood. The focus of civil concepts of parenthood has moved in recent years from biological to functional parenthood. The classic, traditional approach towards parenthood is based on formal, noncontingent definitions.[2] Well-known legal, social, and cultural transitions, as well as scientific developments, led to dramatic structural changes within the family, including the rise of multiple family types and numerous conceptualizations (and resulting definitions) of parenthood: psychological parenting, the actual practicing parents (*de facto* parenting), contract-based parenting, and so on.[3]

One important and widely used concept is functional parenthood. This concept is usually used for defining parenthood based on *ex post* relationships between the child and his or her parents. In this respect, it includes psychological parenthood and other related definitions, while parenthood on the basis

---

1 This part focusses on the conceptual dimensions of ART in Israeli law and their relationships to Jewish law. It is based on my paper: Avishalom Westreich, *Changing Motherhood Paradigms: Jewish Law, Civil Law, and Society*, 28 HASTINGS WOMEN'S L.J. 97 (2017).

2 *See, e.g.*, Nancy D. Polikoff, *This Child Does Have Two Mothers: Redefining Parenthood to Meet the Needs of Children in Lesbian-Mother and Other Nontraditional Families*, 78 GEO. L.J. 459, 468–73 (1990).

3 *See* Polikoff, *id.* at 483–91; Marsha Garrison, *Law Making for Baby Making: An Interpretive Approach to the Determination of Legal Parentage*, 113 HARV. L. REV. 835, 842 (2000) (an approach based on "society's actual practices and beliefs"). For additional discussion and further references, *see* Richard F. Storrow, *Parenthood by Pure Intention: Assisted Reproduction and the Functional Approach to Parentage*, 53 HASTINGS L.J. 597 (2002); Pamela Laufer-Ukeles & Ayelet Blecher-Prigat, *Between Function and Form: Towards a Differentiated Model of Functional Parenthood*, 20 GEO. MASON L. REV. 419, 422, 428–38 (2013). For a recent criticism of these approaches, *see* Scott FitzGibbon, *The Biological Basis for the Recognition of the Family*, 3 INT'L J. JURISPRUDENCE FAM. 1 (2012).

of prenatal agreement or on the basis of the intention of the parties involved may be defined differently.[4] In any event, definitions are quite flexible, and not always agreed; they rather vary between scholarly writings.[5] In general, however, all refer to the nontraditional concepts of parenthood and nontraditional parent-child relations.

For this part's purpose, I will define the whole range of contingent factors of parenthood as a functional approach (in its broader sense).[6] My concept of "functional parenthood" does not merely refer to the actual parenting (that is, functioning as parents) but also to the functionality of the idea, that is, the variety of meanings of parenthood and their use in different functionalities. To be sure, choosing this definition is not due to a decisive argument in the conceptual debate (if such an argument can be made at all). Rather, I chose this definition more for instrumental purposes, for simplifying the discussion, as this definition (the broad meaning of functional parenthood) enables us to clarify more sharply the differentiation of the relatively new approach in Jewish law from the more classic formal-substantive one.

To summarize this point, functional parenthood in my discussion includes psychological parenthood, *de facto* parenthood, contractual parenthood, and every other contingent factor, either *ex ante* or *ex post*, which is beyond the definition of parenthood on the basis of the biological process of reproduction and birth. An agreement between the parties, for example, is a factor external to the process of fertilization and birth, but one that still can influence the legal definition of parenthood, and therefore is defined here as part of a functional approach, rather than a formal one. No less important, the functional definition of parenthood is contingent on the specific legal question. That is, defining parenthood varies from one legal area to the other; for one legal purpose, the parent may be individual X, and for another, Y. In short, this is a functional approach.

4 Laufer-Ukeles & Blecher-Prigat (*id.*) accordingly *see* intentional parenthood as part of formal parenthood. Yehezkel Margalit defines it as "legal parenthood by agreement." *See* Yehezkel Margalit, *Intentional Parenthood: A Solution to the Plight of Same-Sex Partners Striving for Legal Recognition as Parents*, 12 WHITTIER J. CHILD & FAM. ADV. 39, 41 (2013). I would prefer to include it in functional parenthood. *See infra.*

5 In addition to the articles cited above, *see*—on the flexibility of "natural parenthood"—Alison Diduck, *'If Only We Can Find the Appropriate Terms to Use the Issue Will Be Solved': Law, Identity and Parenthood*, 19 CHILD & FAM. L. Q. 458 (2007), and *see* further, the next note.

6 Richard Storrow expands the definition of functional parenthood to include intentional parenthood as well, an approach that I adopt here. *See* Storrow, *supra*, note 3, at 602, 677–678.

II *Israeli Family Law Concepts of Parenthood: Considerate Functionalism*

Israeli law adopts a nonformal (or: intentional-functional) approach regarding the concept of motherhood, that is, defining motherhood according to the context of the case, its circumstances, and, mainly, the intentions of the parties which are reflected in the agreement between them. According to this approach, a child born out of the very same medical process—for example, in vitro fertilization involving two women, a genetic mother (the egg owner) and a gestational mother—could be defined differently, according to the intent of the participants and the agreement between them. In the case of egg donation, the mother will be the gestational mother; while in a case of surrogacy, the mother will be the genetic mother.[7] There is, however, some tendency to viewing the carrying mother as the child's mother, which has consequences for defining motherhood in some exceptional cases: in egg donation, the gestational mother is immediately (right after birth) considered as the legal mother of the child. In surrogacy, on the other hand, the egg owner's motherhood depends on a parenthood decree given by the court, and if there is a significant change in the circumstances, the surrogate mother has the option to rescind her agreement and keep the child, even against the surrogacy contract.[8] The partial bias in favor of the carrying mother may be a result of one or more of the following reasons: first, the practical fact that the child is in the "hands" of the carrying mother (who gave birth of him or her), which leads to the need for an active legal and physical act of giving the child to the genetic mother; second, a (natural?) substantive tendency towards defining the carrying mother as the child's mother; Third, the influence of Jewish law's dominant view (at least at the time those laws were enacted).[9] In any event, this inclination does not change the picture as a whole: the definition of motherhood is still very flexible, and is dependent on the reality and the legal circumstances, so that in most cases (and this is encouraged by the law), the agreements between the parties and their intentions is the definitive, or at least dominant, element

---

7 *See* Egg Donation Law, section 42a; Embryo Carrying Agreements Law, section 11. It should be noted, that basing parenthood on the intention of the parties was proposed by Pinhas Shifman a few years before the enactment of these laws. *See* PINHAS SHIFMAN, FAMILY LAW IN ISRAEL 2, 131–33 (1989).

8 *See* Egg Donation Law, *ibid.*; Embryo Carrying Agreements Law, sections 11–14. For an analysis of this difference, and a proposal for an alternative relational theory for family relations, *see* Ruth Zafran, *The Family in the Genetic Era—Defining Parenthood in Families Created Through Assisted Reproduction Technologies as a Test Case*, 2 DIN UDVARIM 223, 265–68 (2005) (Heb.).

9 Jewish law's view on motherhood will be discussed below.

in defining who is the child's mother.[10] Functional parenthood, thus, is the best definition of the attitude of Israeli law towards children born by assisted reproductive technologies.

Israeli civil law does not adopt a substantive view of parenthood (and in particular, in surrogacy and egg donation cases, of motherhood), that is, a view which coherently follows either the genetic connections or the physical ones. As we have seen, in a surrogacy agreement the mother will be the genetic mother, while in an egg donation the mother will be the carrying mother. But civil law's functionalist approach does not only depend on the circumstances of the case, it also takes into account legal-policy considerations, that is, the view of Jewish law in the matter discussed. From this respect, I would define civil law's approach as "considerate functionalism." We will now explore this idea.

As already mentioned, Jewish law is a central positive source of family law, and significantly influences Israeli civil law.[11] Similarly in our case: Jewish law is often viewed as taking a substantive approach regarding motherhood (I will challenge this view later). Within this approach, however, the decisors debate whether Jewish law follows the genetic connections, in which case the child's mother is the egg owner, or a biological-physical connection, and, consequently, the child's mother will be the carrying mother. We find various approaches on this matter: some decisors argue in favor of the first, some in favor of the second, and others (often due to their doubt regarding the identity of

10 Interestingly, according to a 2013 family court decision (whose view seems to be accepted by the state, that did not appeal) in an international surrogacy (when the surrogate mother does not have any connection to her child, neither by her intention nor by the local law), the court can declare the (Israeli) egg owner as the child's mother based on a judicial decree, and there is no need for the formal process of a motherhood decree (*see* Family Court File [Tel Aviv] 21170-07-12 *Ploni and Almonit v. Attorney General*). This is a result of the fact that Israeli law regulates only local surrogacy, and (still) keeps silent regarding international surrogacy; *see* Yehezkel Margalit, *From Baby M to Baby M(anji): Regulating International Surrogacy Agreements*, 24 J.L. & Pol'y 41, 87–89 (2015). Accordingly, slightly different than the bias in favor of the carrying mother described above, the status of the genetic mother in this case is stronger than that of the surrogate, but this is due to the social and legal context of the case: international, not regulated and unsupervised, surrogacy, which removes the surrogate mother from the picture. It is undoubtedly problematic, and many (including the court in that case) consistently call for legislation on this matter, as well.

11 *See supra*, Part 1.

the mother)—argue for both, or for none.[12] But in any event, the arguments are usually substantive, and if one adopts a particular view, it will be applied to all relevant legal areas and all cases. In this respect, although there is no final decision, we can identify the dominant trend among many, if not the majority, of Jewish law decisors. Rabbi Dr. Mordechai Halperin claims that in the past, most decisors have defined the carrying mother as the child's mother, while today, many of them rule in favor of the genetic one.[13] This is reflected, for example, in the unequivocal decision of the former Israeli Chief Rabbi, Shlomo Amar, that the genetic mother is considered the child's mother for all halakhic matters. Rabi Amar based this ruling, *inter alia*, on a decision by Rabbi Ovadiah Yosef, who was considered the most prominent and leading Jewish law decisor at the turn of the twenty-first century (died 2013).[14] Others, however, are still in doubt,[15] but in any event, *prima facie* all adopt a substantive approach towards parenthood concepts.

Israeli civil law takes into consideration the view of Jewish law in defining motherhood. It does so by subordinating its contingent, functional approach to the view of Jewish law in relevant matters. Thus, the law states explicitly that regarding marriage and divorce (issues that in Israel are subject to religious

12 For a broad discussion and references, *see* MORDECHAI HALPERIN, MEDICINE, NATURE AND HALACHA 278–98 (2011) (Heb.).

13 *Id.* at 294–95. As predicted by Daniel Sinclair: "only the future will tell whether the *halakhah* will move towards a more genetically friendly definition or not." *See* DANIEL SINCLAIR, JEWISH BIOMEDICAL LAW: LEGAL AND EXTRA-LEGAL DIMENSIONS 108 (2003) (*henceforth*: SINCLAIR, JEWISH BIOMEDICAL).

14 *See* a response by Rabbi Shlomo Amar to Prof. Richard V. Grazi (the Director of the Division of Reproductive Endocrinology at Maimonides Medical Center, Brooklyn, NY), *Laws of Pedigree When the Mother Is a Non-Jew*, 87–88 ASSIA 100, 100–102 (2010) (Heb.).

15 This was argued even regarding the view of Rabbi Ovadiah Yosef (in contrast with Rabbi Amar's claim that he decided in favor of the genetic mother); *see* Rabbi Aryeh Katz, *The Parentage of the Embryo from Egg Donation*, 99–100 ASSIA 101, 101–6 (2015) (Heb.), according to whom Rabbi Yosef somewhat shifted to preferring the genetic mother, but did not make a final decision. It should be noted that Rabbi Prof. David Bleich claims that Halperin's description of the present trend among the majority of halakhic decisors is not accurate. Bleich's own view is that either the carrying mother is the sole mother or both the carrying and the genetic ones are the child's mothers (private conversation at the 8th International Academy for the Study of the Jurisprudence of the Family Symposium on "The Jurisprudence of Family Relations," Ono Academic College, Israel, June 9, 2015; and *see* also *infra* note 28).

law),[16] its parenthood definitions will not affect the religious laws.[17] Thus, for example, in surrogacy, after a parenthood decree is issued, the genetic mother is defined as the child's mother for all legal and social purposes (including the child being her heir when the time comes), but for marriage and divorce, the surrogate mother may be defined as the child's mother (thus, this child would be prohibited from marrying the surrogate mother's direct relatives), if that would be the decision of the relevant rabbinical court. The opposite case is also possible: in an egg donation case, the child will be legally and socially considered as the couple's child for any parents-child rights and duties. But when the child wishes to get married, the law (which in this case is subject to Jewish law) may view him or her as the egg donor's child, if that would be the dominant view among Jewish law decisors (as some claim that it is today). As is clear from these examples, this is not only a matter of definition; there are several practical consequences of defining the genetic mother as the mother according to Jewish law, mainly, prohibiting the child from marrying his or her mother's direct relatives (although in this case, due to genetic ties, such a marriage would not be recommended anyway, on both societal and medical grounds).

It should be noted that the interaction between civil law and Jewish law regarding artificial procreation is not limited to conceptual definitions and their halakhic implications. Another aspect of the influence of Jewish law on Israeli civil law is the restrictions due to religious considerations which are imposed on couples and singles who desire assisted procreation. These restrictions limit the available options for assisted procreation. In this respect I would even say that Israeli civil law is not only influenced by but also deferential (perhaps out of fear, if we were to use more critical terminology) to Jewish law.

This is most clearly evident in the preference, and sometimes demand, that a surrogate mother or an egg donor will belong to the same religion as that of the intended parents, as discussed in Part 1.[18] In fact, in surrogacy, the demand that the surrogate mother and the intended parents will belong to the same religion is somewhat stricter than in egg donation: the Egg Donation

16 *See, supra,* Part 1, text accompanying note 32.

17 *See* Embryo Carrying Agreements Law, section 12(b); Egg Donation Law, section 42(b). Both laws state that they will not affect the religious laws of marriage and divorce. The Egg Donation Law also adds that it will not affect the authority of the religious courts (in matters of marriage and divorce): "This law shall not harm the instructions of the laws governing marriage and divorce, or the authority of the religious courts."

18 *See* Embryo Carrying Agreements Law, section 2(5); Egg Donation Law, section 13(e)(3)(a) and 13(e)(4); *supra,* Part 1, section 11 C.

Law provides “after the fact” legitimacy to bypass this demand, if the ova were already taken, as opposed to the Embryo Carrying Agreements Law.[19] This might be a reflection of the inclination towards viewing the carrying mother (i.e., the surrogate mother) as the child's mother, therefore the law ensures that the child given to his or her intended parents will belong to their religion (that is, that the surrogate mother belongs to the same religion). Since, however, this is a matter of religious law, if Jewish law were to change and define the genetic mother as the child's mother (as seems to be the case), this would need to be amended (since if the egg owner is the child's mother, the religion of the surrogate mother does not affect the religion of the child). Anyway, the views among Jewish law decisors vary, and in practice many will insist upon the child's conversion, if either the genetic mother or the carrying mother are not Jewish, in order to circumvent any possible halakhic problem or dispute relating to the child's religious identity.[20]

In my opinion, the considerate functionalism of civil law regarding parenthood concepts should be encouraged in order to reconcile these two legal systems. The practical limitations, however, should be discouraged. Those are matters of personal choice (mainly, whether to involve a partner from another religion in the process of procreation), and therefore should be left to the sole discretion of the parties.

III *Jewish Law Concepts of Parenthood in the Israeli Context*

We saw above the interaction between Jewish law and civil law in one direction: Jewish law's influence on Israeli civil law. Accordingly, some civil elements in the Israeli legal system are based on Jewish law principles; some legal concepts are defined with consideration of, or in accordance with, Jewish law; and in general, the legislator tries to avoid decisions that contradict Jewish law. But is this a mutual interaction, that is, can we find influence in the opposite direction, that of civil law on Jewish law? In what follows, I will seek to reveal a unique conceptual interaction between the two systems: not only a (local) conceptual change, but also what may be seen as the initial signs of a deep paradigmatic change.

In order to support my argument, we will return to the definition of motherhood. Israeli civil law, as argued above, adopts a functional approach regarding motherhood. Therefore, it does not make any clear decision about the identity of the child's mother, whether the genetic mother or the gestational one. Rather, the civil law rulings are flexible and dependent on the circumstances.

19 *See ibid.*

20 *See* Katz, *supra*, note 15.

Jewish law, on the other hand, seeks a substantive definition of motherhood. Therefore, Jewish law decisors attempt to make a conceptual determination of parenthood between the two possible mothers: the genetic one and the carrying one, as well as between them and two other complex options: both or none. About three decades ago, most authorities supported the definition of the carrying mother as the mother according to Jewish Law. But—as Rabbi Dr. Mordechai Halperin argues—this trend has changed, and today many, if not most, argue in favor of the genetic mother.[21] In Amar's case mentioned above, there was a societal need that influenced the move towards the genetic mother.[22] I assume, however, that there is a more general reason that also influences this trend. The move towards the genetic mother might be a result of the development of scientific knowledge of the genetic influence on human nature, that became established and widespread knowledge among the general public, as well. Genetics, thus, could not be ignored, and its legal weight from the point of view of halakhic decisors became more and more significant.

Having made this observation, I admit that no decisive ruling has been issued. Even those who came to lean toward the genetic mother, including Rabbis Ovadiah Yosef and Yosef S. Elyashiv,[23] did not make a decisive conclusion (at least according to some of their close disciples).[24] Not deciding is important here. It opens the gates for accepting various definitions of motherhood within Jewish law itself, and from here—the way is open for a functional definition of motherhood, at least in practice, despite the usual quest for substantive definitions.[25]

---

21 *See supra*, text accompanying notes 12–15. For further discussion of the view of Jewish law decisors on parenthood, *see* A Yehuda Warburg, *Collaborative Reproduction: Unscrambling the Conundrum of Legal Parentage*, 57 And You Shall Surely Heal (Jonathan Wiesen, ed., 2009).

22 *See supra*, note 14. This case and its implication is discussed further *infra*, Part 4.

23 Both are deemed the most prominent halakhic decisors of the twenty-first century. Until their death a few years ago, they were halakhic and political leaders of large religious communities: R. Yosef of the Sephardic Orthodox and traditional community, and R. Elyashiv, of ultra-Orthodox Ashkenazic Jewry.

24 Regarding Rabbi Yosef, *see supra*, note 15. On Rabbi Elyashiv's opinion, *see* Halperin, *supra*, note 12 at 294 note 12.

25 Noam Zohar pointed on initial signs of the move from natural parenthood to parenthood by consent in respect to the approval by a few Jewish law decisors of artificial insemination by donor to a married woman and the resulted change in fatherhood definitions. *See* Noam Zohar, Alternatives in Jewish Bioethics 69–84 (1997). The current analysis, in a 20 years later perspective, reveals a more far reaching trend of moving from natural (or substantial) motherhood to various kinds of functional motherhood (including

The shift towards a functional approach in Jewish law discourse can be found, in my opinion, in four gradual stages:[26]

1. Some did make a decisive ruling, without any flexibility. Rabbi Shlomo Amar, for example, views the genetic mother as the unquestionable child's mother for all halakhic matters.[27] Nevertheless, many still have doubts, and the very existence of doubt is meaningful: it leads to recognizing, at least in principle, the possibility of several mothers of one child.[28] Already in the early discussions on surrogacy, the debate among halakhic decisors led some to claim that both should be treated as the child's mothers, at least as a matter of doubt.[29] Rabbi Yaakov Ariel makes the shift from doubt to double motherhood in a quite poetic way:

> It is written in the book *Nishmat Avraham* [...] in the name of Rabbi. S. Z. Auerbach, of blessed memory, that the status of a child born to a surrogate mother is doubtful, and that we are to apply to him the stringencies that apply to both mothers, his genetic mother and his birth mother. It seems that also in terms of natural feelings—both have maternal

---

motherhood by consent), as regards to motherhood definitions in surrogacy and egg donation.

26 These stages are not chronological. At least the first two coexist. Yet, distinguishing between them clarifies the move to a functional approach. In this respect, at least part of it can be defined as a horizontal process rather than a vertical one.

27 *See supra*, text accompanying note 14.

28 Rabbi Prof. David Bleich already raised this option in 1977; *see* J. David Bleich, Contemporary Halakhic Problems 108 (Vol. 1, 1977). In 1998, however, he preferred the surrogate mother, and even defined her as "a natural mother, both biologically and psychologically." *See* J. David Bleich, *Survey of Recent Halakhic Periodical Literature*, 32 Tradition 146, 162–63 (1998), and similarly in J. David Bleich, Bintivot ha-Halakhah 48 (2000) (Heb.). Later, however, he set forth a more complex position. In a private conversation (*supra*, note 15) Rabbi Bleich explained that, in his opinion, the carrying mother is at least *a mother*. She may be the only mother (as in the classic view), but it is possible that the genetic mother is *also* a mother, and both are defined as the child's mothers. For an analysis of wide range of views, including Bleich and other complex opinions, *see* Benjamin J. Samuels, How Advances in Science Change Jewish Law and Ethics: Assisted Reproductive Technologies and the Redefinition of Parenthood, Part II (Ph.D. Thesis, Boston University, 2017).

29 *See* Halperin, *supra*, note 12 at 295 regarding the view of Rabbi S. Z. Auerbach.

> feelings toward the fetus. The halakhah, that attributes the fetus to both, also corresponds to their natural feelings.[30]

Ariel opens his statement with a doubt regarding the child's mother, but suddenly, based on the two existing views (although they are originally alternative views) and on his assumption of the natural feelings of the women involved in the process, he defines them both as mothers.

Referring to both women as the child's mothers is the first conceptual stage. It undermines the traditional substantive definition of motherhood that has one single mother (in addition to one single father). It also opens the way for the next conceptual stage—"motherhood forum shopping."

2. The very existence of various views makes the definition of motherhood quite flexible. The plurality of opinions enables a kind of forum shopping between the main decisors, in which all the definitions might possibly be valid. Although some would claim that the existence of doubt leads to stringency (at least in matters which are considered more serious, like issues of marriage and divorce), this is not always so. In exceptional cases, it might be possible to rule leniently on the basis of the case's extenuating circumstances, and to follow the view according to which the required act is permitted. For example, if a couple desires a child and must use a surrogate mother, some say that they may do so in practice, despite the objecting Jewish law views and despite the views according to which the child will not be considered the genetic mother's child. For example, Rabbi Zalman Nehemya Goldberg rules that the surrogate mother is the child's mother.[31] He nevertheless acknowledges that there is no agreement among halakhic decisors in this matter, and therefore, as a matter of doubt, both the genetic and carrying mothers should be treated as the child's mothers for matters of marriage and divorce.[32] Yet, in practice, he permits a childless couple to use surrogacy (even though in his opinion the child would not be considered as the genetic mother's child).[33]

30 Rabbi Yaacov Ariel, *Artificial Procreation and Surrogacy*, 16 TECHUMIN 171, 178 (1996) (Heb.).

31 *See* Rabbi Zalman N. Goldberg, *Attribution of Motherhood in the Implanting of a Fetus in the Womb of Another Woman*, 5 TECHUMIN 248 (1984) (Heb.); Rabbi Zalman N. Goldberg, *Maternity in Fetal Implant*, 1 CROSSROADS 71 (1987).

32 *See* Zalman N. Goldberg, *On Egg Donation, Surrogacy, Freezing the Sperm of a Single Man, and Extracting Sperm from a Corpse: Response to the Committee for the Approval of Agreements for Carrying Fetuses by Rabbi Zalman Nehemiah Goldberg*, 65–66 ASSIA 45 (1999) (Heb.).

33 *See id.*

Thus, the second conceptual stage of the shift from substantive motherhood to a functional one is the legitimization of a kind of forum shopping in the status of the mothers. This, in turn, leads to a deeper functionalism regarding motherhood, as we will now explore.

3. The third (conceptual) stage is the use of different criteria for defining the mother of a child in different legal realms, while recognizing each of these criteria as legitimate and valid. Some decisors claim that the two mothers can coexist, depending on which Jewish law question is under discussion. Thus, for instance, for matters of marriage and divorce, the mother may be the genetic mother; for matters of daily life (which are governed by certain religious commandments, such as "Honor your father and your mother"—Exodus 20:12), the mother may be the carrying mother; and for matters of religious identity, the mother might be neither (depending on the specific case).[34] This stage is important, since it enables the coexistence of two mothers: one mother satisfies one group of criteria for one halakhic aspect; and the other, a second group of criteria for a second legal aspect. Clearly, this makes the definition of motherhood much more flexible. It theoretically (or ideally) assumes substantive motherhood, but the fact that motherhood varies from one realm to another, even for the same child, makes it quite contingent, and close to what may be defined as a functional approach.

4. What is missing for a full functional approach is motherhood being dependent not only on the *issue* discussed (i.e., on the halakhic realm—a question that still has ties to substantive motherhood) but also on its *circumstances*. The circumstances in this context may include not only realistic, social circumstances, but also the position of civil law (which, from a halakhic point of view, does not *a priori* affect the substantive halakhic arena).

The fourth stage, in which the definition of motherhood becomes dependent on civil law and on social circumstances, hence represents a (full) functional approach. By this stage, the incremental process of a paradigmatic shift of the halakhic discourse from a substantive understanding of motherhood to a functional one is completed. This stage is quite revolutionary from a Jewish law perspective, and is represented less in explicit fashion and more in subtext. Its appearance is not yet completed, we rather have what can be defined as the

---

34 *See* Rabbi Luz's opinion, *infra* note 37. Rabbi Yechiel M. Stern adopts a similar approach, that is, that motherhood varies from one legal issue to another, but contrary to Rabbi Luz, he prefers to define the genetic mother as a mother for matters of "Honor your father and your mother"; *see* Yechiel M. Stern, *Halakhic Aspect*, FIRST ANNUAL CONFERENCE FOR RABBIS AND PHYSICIANS ON GYNECOLOGY, FERTILITY, & FETUSES ACCORDING TO HALAKHAH 138, 140 (1992) (Heb.).

initial signs for that change. My expectations, however, due to the direction in which the halakhic discourse is developing, as described above, is that this approach will have a greater presence.

Is this approach really to be found? In a fascinating verdict, a regional rabbinical court seems to have made this step. The court, for certain purposes, linked the halakhic definition of motherhood with the civil definitions. This occurred in the following case: according to Jewish law, if a widow has a baby she cannot remarry until the baby is 24 months old. The object of this law is to protect the baby from being abandoned or not being fed if his or her mother will remarry.[35] Without getting into a detailed discussion of this law, its assumptions, and the relevancy of its underlying reason, it is still binding today, although not on a high level in the normative scale of Jewish law (that is, its authority is only that of a rabbinical law rather than Biblical).[36] Nevertheless, the fact that we speak here about a lower normative level is fertile ground for the development of such a significant change in the attitude towards motherhood.

This ruling was issued in a case brought to the Beer-Sheba regional rabbinical court. The judge (Rabbi Zion Luz) permitted a divorced surrogate mother to remarry, even without the 24-month waiting period from the child's birth. He based his decision on several arguments, including the following two: first, that the definition of motherhood varies from case to case, and is in fact contingent on the specific issue. It is possible that for one issue the genetic mother will be deemed the mother, and at the same time, for another issue, the surrogate mother will be so considered. Therefore, for the purpose of this specific law, the surrogate mother is not considered as the mother at all, and that requirement would not be applied to her (the third conceptual level).[37] Second, since according to Israeli civil law, the intended parents are the baby's parents for any civil purposes (on the basis of the surrogacy agreement between them and the surrogate mother) and after a legal parenthood decree has been issued it cannot be changed, the 24-month waiting period law is not relevant here.[38]

In the first argument, Rabbi Luz states that there are different criteria for defining the mother in different legal realms, thereby reflecting the third stage

35 *See* Babylonian Talmud, Yevamot 42a.

36 Therefore, there is room for leniency. *See, e.g.*, File No. 1048925/1 Rabbinical Court (Ashkelon), *Plonit (petitioner)*, (Dec. 3, 2015), Nevo Legal Database (Heb.) (Isr.), in which the rabbinical court permitted a woman whose husband died by a terror attack to remarry, even though she had a very young child.

37 *See* File No. 1014227/2 Rabbinical Court (Beer Sheva), *Ploni v. Plonit*, (May 25, 2015), Nevo Legal database (Heb.) (Isr.).

38 *Id.*; the relevant law is the Embryo Carrying Agreements Law, sections 10–12.

of developing the halakhic functional approach regarding motherhood. The second argument, according to which the decision is influenced by the civil law parenthood decree, is challenging. Is it an independent argument (i.e., that since the law sees the intended mother as the mother, the 24-month waiting period for the surrogate mother is then irrelevant), or is it connected to the first one (i.e., that civil law also influences the halakhic definition of mother, and therefore the waiting period is immaterial)? In my opinion, the second option sounds more plausible (although I admit that the first one is also possible): halakhic motherhood is also influenced by civil definitions. In our case, accordingly, the surrogate mother is not the child's mother, since civil law fully recognizes the intended parents as the child's parents. In my reading, the first argument is, in fact, the theoretical basis for the second one, that is, the fact that the 24-month waiting period is irrelevant for the surrogate mother (due to the surrogacy civil agreement) leads to defining her as *not a mother for this purpose*, theoretically justified by the plurality of motherhood definitions for different legal realms.

If my reading is correct, we have here a fascinating progression of the concept of functional motherhood. We already know that motherhood changes from case to case (either in a forum shopping model or by the distinction between different legal realms). Here, however, this functionality is taken a step further: for the purpose of the 24-month requirement, the concept of motherhood according to Jewish law is subject to civil definitions, which result from the agreement between the parties and its regulation by civil law. Here, since civil law defines the genetic mother as the only mother, Jewish law follows it and does not define the surrogate mother as the child's mother for this function. It therefore releases the surrogate mother from her obligation to wait before her remarriage.

IV *Conclusions: Functional Parenthood and Conceptual Dynamism*

In conclusion, there is a mutual interaction between Israeli law, Jewish law, and society both in the practical level and in the conceptual level. Jewish law influences civil law—in the cases discussed here: by limiting Israeli law's functional approach and subjecting it in some aspects to religious law. We have accordingly defined Israeli law's approach as "considerate functionalism." Society influences Jewish law—by forcing its decision makers to find legal justifications for common practices (see further next part).

The mutual interaction is however not only in the practical level, but rather can be found also in the conceptual level. According to the analysis proposed in this part, Jewish law's approach changes from a formal-substantive approach to motherhood to a functionalist approach. It might be an internal legal development, but at least part of it is a result of Jewish law's interaction with civil law: in the final stage of the conceptual development, Jewish law shapes its contingent, legal concepts in accordance with and as a result of civil legal definitions.

Part 4 The Modern Right to Procreate: Basic Jewish Law Approaches

I *Background*

The first part of this monograph focused on the right to procreate in Israeli law, taking into consideration also the restrictions imposed on it due to religious law. Religious law accompanied our discussion throughout the other parts as well. This part will complete our discussion by focusing independently on Jewish law, and by this will provide a fuller and comprehensive picture of the central elements that play at the Israeli ART field.[1] What, thus, is the position of Jewish law regarding ART?

There is a wide range of opinions within Jewish law regarding the attitude towards assisted reproductive technologies. There is also a broad spectrum of views in the conceptual discussion of the definitions of parenthood, motherhood, and fatherhood, and the positive discussion of what is permitted or prohibited from a Jewish law perspective is strongly connected to the conceptual discussion. More precisely, there are bilateral relationships, that is: the conceptual discussion both influences and is influenced by the positive discussion of what is permitted and what is prohibited.

The various views were presented and discussed in quite a few scholarly works.[2] Here, we are interested in the basic assumptions of Jewish law towards ART, with a focus on the process of mutual influence and complex interaction between the participants in the discussion of assisted reproductive technologies: civil law, religious law, and society.

---

1 The following discussion is based on my papers: *Changing Motherhood Paradigms* (*supra*, Part 3 note 1), and Avishalom Westreich, *Flexible Formalism and Realistic Foundationalism: An Analysis of the Artificial Procreation Controversy in Jewish Law* 31 Dine Israel 157 (2017) (Heb.), with necessary additions and updates.

2 *See* Mordechai Halperin, Medicine, Nature and Halacha 278–98 (2011) (Heb.); Irshai, *infra*, note 7, at 254–64, Sinclair, *infra* note 3; Zohar, *supra*, chapter 3 note 25; Yechiel M. Barilan, Jewish Bioethics: Rabbinic Law & Theology in their Social & Historical Contexts 123–59 (2014) and more. Some of the sources are discussed in Westreich, *supra*, note 1.

II *Areas of Tension*

On the basis of the discussion in previous parts we could (correctly) expect an apparent openness of Jewish law towards ART. But it was not always so: it was not easy for Jewish law to accept Assisted Reproductive Technologies in their first steps, and in fact, this is not absolutely accepted even today.[3]

The first significant steps in ART were made at the end of the nineteenth century and the beginning of the twentieth century. At that time, it was only the more moderate technology of artificial insemination which was discussed by that time's Jewish law decisors.[4] Despite the fact that artificial insemination, when using the husband's sperm, is very close to the natural process of reproduction, it still faced objections, or at least hesitations, from the decisors.

The first two prominent decisors who discussed the use of artificial insemination in practice have reached quite opposite conclusions. The first, Rabbi Shalom Mordecai Shvadron (1835–1911), permitted (in specific circumstances); the second, Rabbi Malkiel Zvi Tenenbaum (1847–1910) was strict and prohibited the practice. Both, however, raised very similar concerns from a Jewish law perspective, concerns that charted the way for discussions on ART to the present.[5]

A few problems were raised regarding artificial insemination. I will mention two of them. First, regarding the positive Biblical commandment to be fruitful and multiply:[6] does the couple comply with this Biblical commandment when being fertilized artificially, or only when the conception is done naturally? The commandment to be fruitful and multiply is undoubtedly one of the main cultural catalysts of ART from a Jewish perspective[7] (in addition to other historical and cultural factors, such as in the post-World War II period—the restoration

3 *See* Daniel Sinclair, *Assisted Reproduction in Jewish Law*, 30 FORDHAM URB. L.J. 71 (2002); SINCLAIR, JEWISH BIOMEDICAL, *supra*, Part 3 note 13, at 68–120.

4 The first reported case of artificial insemination in humans was in 1799, but its wide use started only in the first decades of the twentieth century. *See* Allen D. Holloway, *Artificial Insemination: An Examination of the Legal Aspects*, 43 A.B.A. J. 1089, 1089–90 (1957). Jewish law decisors already raised the option of artificial insemination in the medieval period, but only theoretically. *See, e.g.*, RESPONSA TASHBETZ, 3:263; Simcha Emanuel, *Pregnancy Without Sexual Relations in Medieval Thought*, 62 J.J.S. 105 (2011). Its practical use was discussed at the end of the nineteenth century or at the beginning of the twentieth century (the exact dates are missing), quite close to the beginning of its wider use in the world; *see* below.

5 *See* RESPONSA MAHARSHAM, 3:268 (1962); RESPONSA DIVREI MALKI'EL, 4:107–8 (2001).

6 *Genesis* 1:28. This is considered to be the first commandment that God gave to humans. According to Jewish law, it is fulfilled when the couple has two children: one boy and one girl. *See* Maimonides, MISHNEH TORAH, *Ishut* (Marital Relations) 15:4.

7 On the religious status and importance of the commandment to be fruitful and multiply as a basis for the discussion of procreation (including artificial procreation) from a feminist view,

of the Jewish people after the Holocaust).[8] But is the commandment fulfilled in those ways? The question of parenthood, or more precisely: who is defined as a father, is obviously crucial here: if the genetic father is not deemed the child's father, he then does not comply with this commandment. Second, regarding a negative commandment: Jewish law objects to masturbation (and other ways of "destruction of seed" not in sexual relationships), and sperm extraction is considered forbidden, as well. Some may expand this prohibition even if the act is performed for artificial insemination. The way of defining parenthood concepts (and fatherhood, in this case, in particular) is crucial here, since it influences the question of whether it is considered masturbation or not.

More developed and sophisticated technologies raise more complex problems.[9] In the case of surrogacy and an egg donation, who is defined as the mother of the child? This is not only a theoretical question, it also has important practical implications. For example, if a married surrogate mother is legally (or: halakhically, i.e., from a Jewish law perspective) considered to be the child's mother, the child might be considered as an illegitimate child that was born out of adultery (a *mamzer*; often translated as bastard). According to Jewish law, if a married woman gives birth to a child whose father is not her husband, the child is deemed a *mamzer* and may suffer legal sanctions, mainly the prohibition to wed according to Jewish law.[10] So, is the child born to a married surrogate mother considered her child, and does this result in declaring him or her a *mamzer*?

This point takes us back to artificial insemination. Similar to the discussion regarding a married surrogate mother, in the case of artificial insemination from a donor to a married woman, if the sperm donor is considered as the child's father, is the child (whose father is not the husband of the child's mother) considered to be a *mamzer*?

The discussion does not end with the legal-formal considerations of positive or negative commandments. It also entails metalegal, metaphysical, and religious considerations, such as the legitimacy of human intervention in the Creation and the fear of a "slippery slope" in the use of artificial technologies for that purpose. These types of considerations appear in the discussions by

---

see Ronit Irshai, Fertility and Jewish Law 25–52 (Joel A. Linsider, trans., 2012). For further references, *see* Part 1, note 7.

8 *See* references *ibid.*

9 Sinclair, Jewish Biomedical, *supra*, Part 3 note 13, at 102–109.

10 *See* Maimonides, Mishneh Torah, *Ishut* 1:7; *Issurei Bi'ah* (Forbidden Sexual Relations) 15:1.

twentieth-century Jewish law decisors.[11] My impression, however, is that the metaphysical considerations are of lesser importance than the formal legal arguments or the "slippery slope" considerations, which are more frequently raised in this context.[12]

III *Jewish Law under Societal Pressure*

As mentioned, at the turn of the twentieth century the very moderate ART procedure of artificial insemination encountered resistance by some (but not all) Jewish law decisors (for example, Rabbi Malkiel Tenenbaum). Some did approve, but with limitations (for example, Rabbi Shalom M. Shvadron). All were concerned by various problems, including legal and metalegal issues, and questions of halakhic policy.

These hesitations continue to the present, but it seems that on the issue of artificial procreation practice triumphs over theory (certainly regarding artificial insemination, but also regarding more developed technologies, such as IVF, and even regarding surrogacy and egg donation). Assisted procreation is very common today, even among religious and ultra-Orthodox communities.[13] As a result of this pressure, as we will show, most Jewish law decisors approve ART in practice, including some of its strongest opponents.

For example, Rabbi Moshe Sternbuch, an ultra-Orthodox leader and the head of a well-known (private) rabbinical court, the *Edah Haredit* court, was throughout the years a strict opponent of assisted reproductive technologies. Nevertheless, regarding artificial insemination or IVF he admitted:

> I could discuss this further but [...] here I shall stop writing and the chooser will choose [...] since I and those who are like me are not eligible to decide. And I think that if someone is lenient [and permits ART] he has what to base [his leniency] on, and we should not protest against him.[14]

Rabbi Sternbuch preferred at this stage a silent acceptance of IVF and artificial insemination, although he himself (as is clear from this passage) opposed these techniques. He does so by not answering those who ask him whether the

---

11 *See, e.g.*, Rabbi ELI'EZER WALDENBERG, RESPONSA TSIZ ELI'EZER, 15:45 (1983).

12 For a discussion of the types of considerations in the artificial procreation debate, *see* Westreich, *Flexible Formalism and Realistic Essentialism* (*supra*, note 1).

13 This is probably due to the religious, cultural, and historical causes mentioned above. *See supra*, text accompanying notes 7–8.

14 Rabbi MOSHE STERNBUCH, TESHUVOT VE-HANHAGOT 4:285 (1991–1992).

act is permitted, and thereby hints that if the questioners follow the permissive opinions, he would not object.

In recent years, however, Sternbuch entirely changed his mind, and permitted, even encouraged, the use of ART for married couples. As he writes: "when I saw that the practice was spread ... I changed my mind, and now I think that ... a child born through IVF is surely considered the child of the sperm owner", who by this complies with the commandment of to be fruitful and multiply.[15] This astonishing change occurred due to the fact that IVF and artificial insemination have become common even among religious communities, and it led R. Sternbuch first to a pragmatic decision, and then to a full approval of the practice.

Social practice, however, does not always win out in Sternbuch's writings. When it crosses some borders (for example, in surrogacy, or when artificial insemination involves the participation of both Jews and non-Jews, due to the Orthodox sensitivity regarding interfaith family ties), he objects, even in the face of societal pressure, despite the fact that "it has become common even within the ultra-Orthodox communities."[16]

In current reality, however, the vast majority of the prominent Jewish law decisors, do accept the wider ART practices, even in those cases that seem to cross more basic halakhic or metahalakhic borders (such as involving a married woman as a surrogate mother while using the sperm of the intended father, who is not her husband).[17] They would not *a priori* recommend this, but when they recognize the specific need of the couple, they would approve various ART procedures, even the more complex and problematic (from a Jewish law perspective) among them.

For example, Rabbi Shlomo Amar's 2006 decision that permitted a couple childless after thirteen years of marriage to enter into a surrogacy agreement with a married surrogate mother.[18] As discussed in previous part, the decision is highly innovative because of the explicit permission to use surrogacy, and because of overcoming the traditional fear of involving a third-party married wife in other family relationships, which might lead to declaring the child a *mamzer* according to Jewish law.[19] Rabbi Amar ruled that the genetic mother is considered—without doubt—the child's mother and therefore a married

15 Rabbi MOSHE STERNBUCH, TESHUVOT VE-HANHAGOT 6:241 (2013–2014).

16 Rabbi MOSHE STERNBUCH, TESHUVOT VE-HANHAGOT 5:318, 319 (2008–2009).

17 *See supra*, text accompanying notes 9–10, regarding the fear of declaring the child a *mamzer*.

18 *See supra*, Part 3, text accompanying notes 13–14.

19 *See supra*, text accompanying notes 9–10.

surrogate mother can participate in the process. And although he emphasized that it is permitted only when other options were not possible, as in this specific case, in recent years the use of a married surrogate mother has become more and more common.[20] The somewhat limiting scope of the remark by Rabbi Amar provides us with an interesting insight regarding law and society: it reveals how personal needs and societal pressure lead Jewish law scholars to make lenient decisions regarding ART, and how these decisions affect society by making the practice more widespread and accepted by Jewish law.

Leniency in Rabbi Amar's case ensues from a clear decision on the conceptual debate over motherhood, that is, that the genetic mother is the child's mother (and the only mother of the child). The conjunction between the two aspects (the practical and the conceptual) is not coincidental. Although a married surrogate mother could possibly be approved even if the child would be considered hers, it is much simpler to permit this if the surrogate mother is not considered the child's mother. In the first option, some may fear that the child (born to a married woman from a person other than her husband) is a *mamzer*. Although this fear will probably be rejected, it will still lead to some hesitations regarding approval of surrogacy.[21] In the second option, on the other hand, no such a claim could be raised, since the child is not the surrogate mother's child. Therefore, I assume that Rabbi Amar's conceptual decision was important in order to facilitate permitting surrogacy with the involvement of a married woman.

Similar view regarding motherhood is held by the current Israeli Chief Rabbi, Itshak Yosef (following the decision of his father, Rabbi Ovadiah Yosef, which was adopted by R. Amar as well). Truly, this approach might lead to some difficulties in approving the other option, that of egg donation (since the donor is considered, according to this view, the mother). But R. Yosef approves also egg donation when the couple strongly desire a child. He nevertheless does not ignore the difficulties: he acknowledges that the mother is the egg owner, and therefore if she is not Jewish, the child, raised by the intended Jewish couple, would have to go through a process of conversion. But the whole process, as one could be impressed by reading Yosef's responsum, does not lead

20 *Supra*, Part 1, text accompanying notes 47–48.

21 As already mentioned, the fear will probably be rejected, since according to many halakhic decisors, one is declared a *mamzer* only when the child was born as a result of a forbidden sexual relationship. This is not the case in surrogacy and egg donation, since the child was born without the commission of adultery (i.e., without a sexual relationship between the surrogate mother and the father). *See* RESPONSA MAHARSHAM, 3:268 (1962); Rabbi MOSHE FEINSTEIN, IGGROT MOSHE, *Even Ha-'ezer* 1:10 (1959).

to significant hesitations regarding its application. The basic openness exists, even when it requires to face challenges resulted from conceptual definitions of motherhood and the sensitivity of religious affiliation.[22]

IV *Closing Remarks*

Our discussion in this part began with the practical influence of societal pressure on Jewish law decisors, and it ended with a more far-reaching conclusion: that societal pressure also influences the conceptual approach of Jewish law decisors to the definition of parenthood. The process of conceptual change in Jewish law is quite impressive. This change results from societal pressure, coupled with an internal Jewish law discussion, and reciprocally influences the practical sphere, by widening the possible options of artificial procreation as discussed above.

Jewish law thereby assists in creating a fertile ground for the prevalent use and development of assisted reproduction in Israel. Jewish law, however, is not a single player: it normatively interacts with civil law, and exhibits a careful awareness of scientific developments and social stances. This functional collaboration enables an impressive flourishing of the right to procreate. This right, despite debates on its boundaries, is widely accepted, practiced, and even encouraged in the Israeli context, with a constructive collaboration of three main elements: the Israeli civil legal system, religious law (which in the context of the Israeli majority is Jewish law), and Israeli society and culture.

References

A. *Scholarly References*

Amar, Rabbi Shlomo, *Laws of Pedigree When the Mother Is a Non-Jew (Response to Prof. Richard V. Grazi)*, 87–88 ASSIA 100 (2010) (Heb.).

Ariel, Rabbi Yaacov, *Artificial Procreation and Surrogacy*, 16 TECHUMIN 171 (1996) (Heb.).

Barilan, Yechiel M., JEWISH BIOETHICS: RABBINIC LAW & THEOLOGY IN THEIR SOCIAL & HISTORICAL CONTEXTS (2014).

Bartholet, Elizabeth, *Intergenerational Justice for Children: Restructuring Adoption, Reproduction and Child Welfare Policy*, 8 LAW & ETHICS HUM. RIGHTS 103 (2014).

Blecher-Prigat, Ayelet, *From Partnership to Joint-Parenthood: The Financial Implications of the Joint Parenthood Relationship*, 19 LAW AND BUSINESS—IDC L. REV. 821 (2016) (Heb.).

22 *See* Rabbi ITSHAK YOSEF, RESPONSA HA-RISHON LE-ZION, 5–6 (2016).

Bleich, Rabbi J. David, BINTIVOT HA-HALAKHAH (2000) (Heb.).

Bleich, Rabbi J. David, CONTEMPORARY HALAKHIC PROBLEMS 1 (1977).

Bleich, Rabbi J. David, *Survey of Recent Halakhic Periodical Literature: Posthumous Paternity* 49 TRADITION 72 (2016).

Bleich, Rabbi J. David, *Survey of Recent Halakhic Periodical Literature*, 32 TRADITION 146 (1998).

Bokek-Cohen, Ya'arit, and Ravitsky, Vardit, *Soldiers' Preferences Regarding Sperm Preservation, Posthumous Reproduction, and Attributes of a Potential "Posthumous Mother,"* OMEGA—JOURNAL OF DEATH AND DYING (Published online, August 11, 2017, https://doi.org/10.1177/0030222817725179).

Diduck, Alison, *'If Only We Can Find the Appropriate Terms to Use the Issue Will Be Solved': Law, Identity and Parenthood*, 19 CHILD & FAM. L. Q. 458 (2007).

Emanuel, Simcha, *Pregnancy Without Sexual Relations in Medieval Thought*, 62 J.J.S. 105 (2011).

Evans, Jon B., *Post-mortem Semen Retrieval: A Normative Prescription for Legislation in the United States*, 1 CONCORDIA L. REV. 133 (2016).

FitzGibbon, Scott, *The Biological Basis for the Recognition of the Family*, 3 INT'L J. JURISPRUDENCE FAM. 1 (2012).

Garrison, Marsha, *Law Making for Baby Making: An Interpretive Approach to the Determination of Legal Parentage*, 113 HARV. L. REV. 835, 842 (2000).

Goldberg, Rabbi Zalman N., *Attribution of Motherhood in the Implanting of a Fetus in the Womb of Another Woman*, 5 TECHUMIN 248 (1984) (Heb.).

Goldberg, Rabbi Zalman N., *Maternity in Fetal Implant*, 1 CROSSROADS 71 (1987).

Goldberg, Rabbi Zalman N., *On Egg Donation, Surrogacy, Freezing the Sperm of a Single Man, and Extracting Sperm from a Corpse: Response to the Commission for the Approval of Agreements for Carrying Fetuses by Rabbi Zalman Nehemiah Goldberg*, 65–66 ASSIA 45 (1999) (Heb.).

Goldberg, Rabbi Zalman N., *On Egg Donation, Surrogacy, Freezing the Sperm of a Single Man, and Extracting Sperm from a Corpse: Response to the Committee for the Approval of Agreements for Carrying Fetuses by Rabbi Zalman Nehemiah Goldberg*, 65–66 ASSIA 45 (1999) (Heb.).

Halperin, Rabbi Mordechai, MEDICINE, NATURE AND HALACHA (2011) (Heb.).

Hashiloni-Dolev, Yael, and Triger, Zvi, *Between the Deceased's Wish and the Wishes of His Surviving Relatives: Posthumous Children, Patriarchy, Pronatalism, and the Myth of Continuity of the Seed*, 39 IYUNEI MISHPAT (TAU L. REV.) 661 (2016) (Heb.).

Henshke, David, *Two Subjects Typifying the Tannaitic Halakhic Midrash*, 65 TARBIZ 417 (1996) (Heb.).

Holloway, Allen D., *Artificial Insemination: An Examination of the Legal Aspects*, 43 A.B.A. J. 1089 (1957).

Irshai, Ronit, FERTILITY AND JEWISH LAW (Joel A. Linsider, trans., 2012).

Jackson, Bernard S., *Ruth, the Pentateuch and the Nature of Biblical Law: In Conversation with Jean Louis Ska*, 75 The Post-Priestly Pentateuch: New Perspectives on its Redactional Development and Theological Profiles (Konrad Schmid and Federico Giuntoli eds., 2015).

Katz, Rabbi Aryeh, *The Parentage of the Embryo from Egg Donation*, 99–100 Assia 101 (2015) (Heb.).

Knohl, Rabbi Elyashiv, *Halakhic Positions on Surrogacy* (2016), http://www.tzohar.org.il/?p=7352 (Heb.).

Laufer-Ukeles, Pamela, and Blecher-Prigat, Ayelet, *Between Function and Form: Towards a Differentiated Model of Functional Parenthood*, 20 Geo. Mason L. Rev. 419 (2013).

Margalit, Yehezkel, *From Baby M to Baby M(anji): Regulating International Surrogacy Agreements*, 24 J.L. & Pol'y 41 (2015).

Margalit, Yehezkel, *Intentional Parenthood: A Solution to the Plight of Same-Sex Partners Striving for Legal Recognition as Parents*, 12 Whittier J. Child & Fam. Adv. 39 (2013).

Margalit, Yehezkel, *Scarce Medical Resources—Parenthood at Every Age, In Every Case and Subsidized By the State?*, 9 Netanya Acad. L. Rev. 191 (2014) (Heb.).

Margalit, Yehezkel, *Scarce Medical Resources? Procreation Rights in a Jewish and Democratic State* (2011), http://ssrn.com/abstract=1807908 (unpublished manuscript).

Polikoff, Nancy D., *This Child Does Have Two Mothers: Redefining Parenthood to Meet the Needs of Children in Lesbian-Mother and Other Nontraditional Families*, 78 Geo. L.J. 459 (1990).

Samuels, Benjamin J., How Advances in Science Change Jewish Law and Ethics: Assisted Reproductive Technologies and the Redefinition of Parenthood, Part II (Ph.D. Thesis, Boston University, 2017).

Shafran, Rabbi Ig'al, *Posthumous Fatherhood*, 20 Techumin (2000) (Heb.).

Shalev, Carmel, and Gooldin, Sigal, *The Uses and Misuses of In Vitro Fertilization in Israel: Some Sociological and Ethical Considerations*, 12 Nashim: A Journal of Jewish Women's Studies and Gender Issues 151 (2006).

Shifman, Pinhas, Family Law in Israel 2 (1989).

Sinclair, Daniel, *Assisted Reproduction in Jewish Law*, 30 Fordham Urb. L.J. 71 (2002).

Sinclair, Daniel, Jewish Biomedical Law: Legal and Extra-Legal Dimensions (2003).

Steinberg, Avraham, and Rosner, Fred, Encyclopedia of Jewish Medical Ethics, 695–711 (2003).

Stern, Rabbi Yechiel M., *Halakhic Aspect*, First Annual Conference for Rabbis and Physicians on Gynecology, Fertility, & Fetuses according to Halakhah 138 (1992) (Heb.).

Storrow, Richard F., *Parenthood by Pure Intention: Assisted Reproduction and the Functional Approach to Parentage*, 53 Hastings L.J. 597 (2002).

Warburg, Rabbi A. Yehuda, *Collaborative Reproduction: Unscrambling the Conundrum of Legal Parentage*, 57 AND YOU SHALL SURELY HEAL (Jonathan Wiesen, ed., 2009).

Westreich, Avishalom, and Shifman, Pinhas, A CIVIL LEGAL FRAMEWORK FOR MARRIAGE & DIVORCE IN ISRAEL (Ruth Gavison, ed., Kfir Levy, trans., 2013).

Westreich, Avishalom, *Book Review: Melanie Landau, Tradition and Equality in Jewish Marriage: Beyond the Sanctification of Subordination* 28 NASHIM: A JOURNAL OF JEWISH WOMEN'S STUDIES AND GENDER ISSUES 147 (2015).

Westreich, Avishalom, *Changing Motherhood Paradigms: Jewish Law, Civil Law, and Society*, 28 HASTINGS WOMEN'S L.J. 97 (2017).

Westreich, Avishalom, *Flexible Formalism and Realistic Foundationalism: An Analysis of the Artificial Procreation Controversy in Jewish Law* 31 DINE ISRAEL 157 (2017) (Heb.).

Westreich, Elimelech, *Levirate Marriage in the State of Israel: Ethnic Encounter and the Challenge of a Jewish State*, 37 ISR. LAW REV. 427 (2003–2004).

Zafran, Ruth, *The Family in the Genetic Era—Defining Parenthood in Families Created Through Assisted Reproduction Technologies as a Test Case*, 2 DIN UDVARIM 223 (2005) (Heb.).

Zohar, Noam, ALTERNATIVES IN JEWISH BIOETHICS (1997).

B. *Jewish Law Sources*

a. Bible and Talmud

Genesis 1, 2, 31, 38

Numbers 27

Deuteronomy 25

Ruth 4

1 Chronicles 4

Babylonian Talmud, Tractate Yevamot

b. Rabbinic Literature

Bekhor Shor, Rabbi Joseph, Deuteronomy 25.

Duran, Simeon ben Zemah, RESPONSA TASHBETZ, 3 (1998).

Feinstein, Rabbi Moshe, IGGROT MOSHE, *Even Ha-'ezer* 1 (1959).

Feinstein, Rabbi Moshe, RESPONSA IGGROT MOSHE, *Even Ha-'ezer* 1 (1959).

Kara, Rabbi Joseph, Deuteronomy 25.

Maimonides (Rabbi Moses ben Maimon), MISHNEH TORAH, *Ishut* (Marital Relations).

Maimonides (Rabbi Moses ben Maimon), MISHNEH TORAH, *Issurei Bi'ah* (Forbidden Sexual Relations).

Rashi (Rabbi Shlomo Yitzhaki), Deuteronomy 25.

Schwadron, Shalom Mordechai, RESPONSA MAHARSHAM 3 (1962).

Sternbuch, Rabbi Moshe, TESHUVOT VE-HANHAGOT 4 (1991–1992).

Sternbuch, Rabbi Moshe, TESHUVOT VE-HANHAGOT 5 (2008–2009).
Sternbuch, Rabbi Moshe, TESHUVOT VE-HANHAGOT 6 (2013–2014).
Tenenbaum, Rabbi Malkiel Z., RESPONSA DIVREI MALKI'EL, 4 (2001).
Tur (R. Jacob ben Asher), Introduction to *Arba'ah Turim.*
Waldenberg, Rabbi Eli'ezer, RESPONSA TSIZ ELI'EZER, 15 (1983).
Weiss, Rabbi Itshak Y., RESPONSA MINHAT ITSHAK, 4 (1993).
Yosef, Rabbi Itshak, RESPONSA HA-RISHON LE-ZION, 5–6 (2016).

C. *Israeli Law*

a. Legislation

Brain-Respiratory Death Law, 5768–2008.
Egg Donation Law, 5770–2010.
Embryo Carrying Agreements Law (Approval of the Agreement and the Status of the Child), 5756–1996.
Fallen Soldier's Sperm Retrieval Proposed Legislation, 2017 (Fallen Soldiers' Families Law [Pensions and Rehabilitation] 5710–1950 [Amendment]).
Sperm Banks Proposed Legislation, 2016.

b. Verdicts

Adoption File 22–17 *Plonit and Ploni vs. Attorney General* (September 13, 2017), PsakDin Legal Database (https://www.psakdin.co.il/Court/1464692#.WgXYKdJBoYo) (*Heb.*) (Isr.).
CFH 2401/95 Nahmani v. Nahmani et al. (September 12, 1996) (Isr.) (http://elyon1.court.gov.il/Files_ENG/95/010/024/z01/95024010.z01.HTM).
Family Appeal 45930-11-16 The State of Israel v. Shahar (January 27, 2017) (Heb.) (Isr.).
Family Appeal Request 1118/14 Plonit v. Ministry of Social Affairs and Social Services (April 1, 2015) (Heb.) (Isr.).
Family Appeal Request 1943/17 Shahar v. The State of Israel (August 15, 2017) (Heb.) (Isr.).
Family Appeal Request 4890/14 Plonit v. Plonit (September 2, 2014) (Heb.) (Isr.).
Family Appeal Request 7141/15 Plonit v. Plonit et al. (December 22, 2016) (Heb.) (Isr.).
Family Appeal Request 7141/15 Plonit v. Plonit et al. (December 22, 2016) (Heb.) (Isr.).
Family Appeal Request 7141/15 Plonit v. Plonit et al. (December 22, 2016) (Heb.) (Isr.).
Family Court File (Tel Aviv) 21170–07–12 *Ploni and Almonit v. Attorney General* (2013) (Heb.) (Isr.).
Family Court File 16699–06–13 Shahar v. Attorney General (September 27, 2017) (Heb.) (Isr.).
Family Court File 52940–06–16 G.D. and D.P. v. Attorney General (May 22, 2017) (Heb.) (Isr.).

File No. 1014227/2 Rabbinical Court (Beer Sheva), *Ploni v. Plonit*, (May 25, 2015), Nevo Legal database (Heb.) (Isr.).

File No. 1048925/1 Rabbinical Court (Ashkelon), *Plonit (petitioner)*, (Dec. 3, 2015), Nevo Legal Database (Heb.) (Isr.).

HCJ 781/15 Itay Arad-Pinkas, Yoav Arad-Pinkas et al. v. The Surrogacy Agreements Approval Committee and the Knesset (August 3, 2017) (Heb.) (Isr.).

c. Other Legal Sources

Hacohen, Aviad, opinion submitted in Family Court File 16699-06-13.

Israeli New Family organization "Biological Will", http://www.newfamily.org.il/en/biological-will-precedents-2/.

Knesset Welfare and Health Committee, August 18, 2006 (http://www.knesset.gov.il/protocols/data/rtf/avoda/2006-08-15–01.rtf).

Mor-Yosef Commission: THE PUBLIC COMMISSION FOR THE EVALUATION OF FERTILITY & CHILDBIRTH 33 (2012, Hebrew version available at: http://www.health.gov.il/publicationsfiles/bap2012.pdf).

The Ethics Committee of the Israel Fertility Association (IFA), POSITION PAPER ON THE USE OF SPERM FROM THE DECEASED: THE RECOMMENDATIONS AND CONCLUSIONS OF THE ETHICS COMMITTEE OF THE ISRAEL FERTILITY ASSOCIATION, November 2017.

D. *Media and Other Sources*

Amit, Ami, A private conversation, November 3, 2017.

Bleich, Rabbi J. David, A private conversation, June 9, 2015.

Cherlow, Yuval, *The Characteristic of Sodom?—Response*, SHABBAT—MAKOR RISHON, May 19, 2017, https://tinyurl.com/y8sf5cqh.

Efrati, Ido, "Israel Remains an IVF Paradise as Number of Treatments Rises 11% in 2016," HAARETZ, May 11, 2017 (http://www.haaretz.com/israel-news/.premium-1.788244).

Haim Levinson, *Chief Rabbi: Married Woman Can Be Surrogate* (June 11, 2006, http://www.ynetnews.com/articles/0,7340, L-3261249,00.html).

Resenberg, Shalom, *When a Right Turns Cruel*, SHABBAT—MAKOR RISHON, May 26, 2017, https://tinyurl.com/yanqgqtd.

Rosenberg, Shalom, *A Grandchild without a Father*, SHABBAT—MAKOR RISHON, May 5, 2017, http://preview.tinyurl.com/yc7xahfz.

Sharon, Jeremy, "Supreme Court Prevents Use of Dead Soldier's Sperm," http://www.jpost.com/Israel-News/Supreme-Court-prevents-use-of-dead-soldiers-sperm-486082 (April 4, 2017).

Printed in the United States
By Bookmasters